In memory of
"Dad" Martin
1909-1980

IDENTITY
and
FAITH

IDENTITY
and
FAITH

Youth in a Believers' Church

Maurice Martin

Foreword by S. David Garber

Focal Pamphlet 31

HERALD PRESS
Kitchener, Ontario
Scottdale, Pennsylvania
1981

Canadian Cataloguing in Publication Data

Martin, Maurice, 1946-
    Identity and faith

(Focal pamphlet; 31)
Bibliography: p.
ISBN 0-8361-1979-7

1. Mennonites. 2. Youth - Religious life.
3. Baptism and church membership. I. Title.
II. Series.

BX8121.2.M37   289.7'088055   C81-095038-3

IDENTITY AND FAITH: YOUTH IN A BELIEVERS' CHURCH
Copyright © 1981 by Herald Press, Kitchener, Ont. N2G 4M5
    Released simultaneously in the United States by Herald Press,
    Scottdale, Pa. 15683
Library of Congress Catalog Card Number: 81-82655
International Standard Book Number: 0-8361-1979-7
Printed in the United States of America
Design: Alice B. Shetler

81 82 83 84 85 86 10 9 8 7 6 5 4 3 2 1

Contents

Foreword

In many believers' church congregations parents and teachers are wondering why youth growing up in Christian families are postponing a public profession of faith, with baptism and church membership, until the mid or late teens, or even longer. Other youth ask for baptism but want to delay joining the local congregation. Some parents think their children "feel left out" at communion services; should they be allowed to participate? Should parents bring children of 9 to 11 years for baptism? Should youth members be permitted to vote at congregational meetings?

In *Identity and Faith*, Maurice Martin tackles such questions from a believers' church understanding of the Scripture and the church. He shares insights developed by the social sciences and helps us understand how youth mature and gain the capability of making a "conscious decision" of lifelong commitment to Christ and the church. While children of a Christian parent belong to the family of God (1 Corinthians 7:14), we need to "allow children to be children!" They need to be nurtured and *brought to* Jesus

(Mark 10:13). Youth and adults, however, are able to answer the call of Christ for themselves. They can affirm covenant with God and his people, and help steer the camels in the caravan of the church!

Maurice shared this material with church leaders at a retreat sponsored by the Mennonite Conference of Ontario and the Western Ontario Mennonite Conference. His work was appreciated. Since then he has recast it for wider usefulness in the church at large.

Maurice lures the reader along with stories from his own years of growing up in the church. He writes with the experience of a parent, teacher, and pastor. He has brought theology, church history, psychology, and sociology together in a way that will be helpful to other parents, teachers, and pastors. In addition, any thoughtful church member can find profit and enlightenment from his insights. All members of the church need to join in this ongoing discussion if we are truly going to celebrate God's faithfulness and mercy from generation to generation (Luke 1:50).

S. *David Garber*, Pastor
Hawkesville Mennonite Church
Hawkesville, Ontario

Author's Preface

If someone should ask me how long it took to write this book, I would probably answer "a whole lifetime, so far, and I am not finished with it yet." This book is really an attempt to focus my growing self-understanding. My hope is that by sharing my story and reflecting on it, I shall provide something of use to the Mennonite Church which I have grown to love and to churches of other theological traditions as well. In each chapter I share personal anecdotes to illustrate the issues to be dealt with in that chapter. Then I proceed to reflect on the place of youth in the church from a variety of perspectives: historical, theological, biblical as well as from the perspectives of the social sciences. It may be apparent to the reader that I have not yet integrated all of these perspectives. Sometimes they intersect nicely; but at other times one needs to run on parallel tracks to describe the same experience from various points of view.

Chapter four presented the greatest difficulty in attempting to integrate the terminology of the various disciplines. I have tried to clarify them by shaping and defining the categories to fit our purposes. I felt that the term "crisis conversion" most closely paralleled the New Testament concept of the "new birth." It certainly describes the way this concept has been integrated into the theological terminology in the history of a certain segment of the church. I propose that if we wish to retain the term "the new birth" and also promote a crisis conversion experience, we need to understand more fully the accompanying emotional impact. However, I also suggest that it should be possible to speak of "a conscious decision," without making it synonymous with a crisis conversion. Therefore, I propose a third category for the Mennonite Church's understanding of conversion. Such an understanding lies between the categories of moral-personal conversion predominant in evangelical revivalism, and ethical-moral conversion more typical of the mainline Protestant and Roman Catholic traditions. This is in keeping with our increasing Mennonite self-awareness that we are, in the final analysis, "neither Catholic nor Protestant."

The reader should note also that the categories from the social sciences are meant to be primarily descriptive. Whether we like what the social scientists see is an entirely different matter. It is then up to us, from a biblical and theological perspective, to prescribe what we would like to see happening in the church and with our youth. Although this book attempts to be analytical, it is, in the final sense, a pastoral work. My hope is that it will be useful in that way for those who work and live with youth in the church.

I am grateful for the kind encouragement and assistance of several people in this endeavor: Thank you to my wife, Phyllis, who has always avowed that I have "a way with words." To Ralph Lebold, who more than he realizes, taught me "the language of feelings." To J. C. Wenger, who allowed me to try to integrate the language of feelings with the language of theology in his class at the Associated Mennonite Biblical Seminaries, Elkhart, Indiana. To David Garber, who read my paper for that class and persuaded me that it should be published, and who has taken me seriously as a writer, sometimes more seriously than I took myself. To Harold Bauman, whose careful reading of my manuscript along the way has helped to make it more error-free, and who taught me how to use nonsexist language. To John Miller, who assisted me in understanding Freudian psychoanalysis and offered several helpful insights along the way. And finally, to my family, for giving me my roots, and to my spiritual family at the St. Jacobs Mennonite Church, who nurtured me in the days of my youth.

Maurice Martin, Pastor
Hagerman Mennonite Church
Milliken, Ontario

IDENTITY and FAITH

Youth in a Believers' Church

To understand what a person is, it is necessary always to refer to what he may be in the future, for every state of the person is pointed in the direction of future possibilities.

—Leibnitz

When I was a child, I spoke like a child, I thought like a child, I reasoned like a child; when I became a man, I gave up childish ways. For now we see in a mirror dimly, but then face to face.

—St. Paul

Chapter One

Affirming Our Church Heritage

I was born into a Mennonite family and was raised to be a Mennonite. In 1961 I was fifteen years old. As a child I was visibly impressed by a number of role models in the life of the church. My earliest aspiration was to be a song leader, and then to be a Sunday school teacher. Reading the *Jungle Doctor* series provoked in me visions of being a missionary doctor! Finally I settled on the ministry. Also in the years from six to fifteen, I experienced two significant spiritual awakenings. My grade two Sunday school teacher caused me to consider whether I too would like to be a follower of Jesus. I responded affirmatively in my own shy and somewhat confused way. When I was fourteen, I attended evangelistic meetings featuring Grady Wilson of the Billy Graham Evangelistic Association. I "went forward" one night and received counseling in a back room of the Kitchener Memorial Auditorium. I remember very little of what was said in that room. There was counseling going on all around me, and I was quite nervous.

That year my pastor contacted me and invited me to join

the church membership class. I remember the room it was held in. I do not recall much of the discussion, except the matter of the prayer veiling. I was baptized that year, with about ten others. One dropped out because his father said he was too young. Although he was baptized the following year, I do not think he is part of the Mennonite Church today.

By age fifteen I was a member of the Mennonite Church. Then I discovered that one had to be sixteen before one could vote or help make decisions at church business meetings. When I was seventeen, several of my friends and I determined that we were going to get on board the ship of state in the church. Six of us walked to the front of the auditorium and sat down to take part in the annual business meeting of the St. Jacobs Mennonite Church. We wanted to take ownership in "our church." Now that was hardly as significant as Luther's stand at the Wittenberg door, but for us it meant a great deal. It symbolized for me the stance I was taking in relation to the church of my parents. It was one way for me to trade in the secondhand fittings attached to being "the church of tomorrow," so that I could, in a firsthand way, own my heritage and be an integral part of "the church of today."

This story could be repeated many times with many variations by many members of the Mennonite Church. No doubt the stories that youth tell today have dimensions which I never experienced. But the first step in understanding how youth fit into the life of the Mennonite Church is for us to tell our stories. The second step is to pause to reflect upon what these stories mean. In this chapter and those that follow I shall attempt to focus this reflection from a variety of perspectives: historical, theological, biblical, and from the perspectives of the social sciences. At some points it will be

18

obvious that I have not yet integrated all of these perspectives entirely. Perhaps complete integration can never happen. In any case, it would take more time and space than we have here. For that reason it may appear that we are raising more questions than we are answering. These questions are intended to stimulate further thinking and discussion. The answers that are beginning to focus for me, I shall present as clearly as possible.

In the Mennonite Church today there is considerable confusion about the meaning and nature of baptism and church membership. Many young people are unclear about these and about the nature of Christian experience as such. On every side they are faced with a variety of emphases, often confronted with diverse claims for their allegiance. We no longer, by and large, have the neat formulas on how to become a Christian which we inherited from our church in the previous generation. Then it was accepted as a matter of course that in one's late teens or early twenties, certainly before marriage, one would join the church through the due process of the membership class and agreeing with the eighteen articles of faith. Also, in the past decades, we were certainly influenced by the evangelical revivalist movement in North America. Under that influence, it seemed quite clear what it meant to make a decision for Christ. There were regular opportunities to declare publicly one's decision to become a Christian. In many circles of the Mennonite Church this process was so neatly prescribed that we began to raise the question as to whether one could become a Christian by any other way. Thus in 1954 Gideon Yoder attempted to answer some of these questions in his book, *The Nurture and Evangelism of Children.* Yoder's work is still very pertinent today, and I shall assume many of the helpful ideas which he advanced in his writing.

Today we do not generally give our youth the opportunity to declare publicly their decision for Christ as we did almost regularly at one time. I shall later assess the relative value of this type of event. Here I simply wish to say that we have largely diffused the concept of decisive moments in the Christian walk, beginning with a conscious point of commitment, in favor of a more gradual nurturing into Christian faith. Many of us remember the acute anguish we felt as week by week we had our "spiritual plants" torn up by the roots for examination! We were reminded in glowing terms that we either needed to make our initial commitment to Christ, or we needed to rededicate our lives to him. It took me several years before I could sit through "an invitation" without sweating and hanging on to the pew ahead of me. Many of us walked "the sawdust trail" many times. So, partially to spare our youth that traumatic experience, and for other reasons, we have taken other approaches to calling forth Christian commitment. In many instances, we have hoped that by drawing our young people into church membership classes for catechetical instruction we could bring about a positive decision for Christ and the church. This may in the long run have more solid effects. In the meantime, young people are beginning to postpone church membership, often to their late teens. This is cause for joy to some, but concern for others. The joy is that those who are postponing it are consequently taking it more seriously. The concern is for those who never take a stand for Christ.

If there is, as I have observed, a great deal of confusion on the part of our youth about the nature and meaning of baptism and church membership, let me hasten to say that it is not necessarily their problem alone. They reflect, more than we care to admit, the attitudes of their elders. On the one hand, we have parents who are quite anxious about their children. Their question is "will our children have faith?" One reason the question is raised is that the parents themselves do not always feel equipped to lead their children to faith. They would feel much more comfortable knowing that the church will do this for them. But they no longer see the visible public efforts in that direction and therefore assume that it is not happening. They are very concerned then, if their children become teenagers before they have accepted the Christian way and baptism. This type of parental anxiety has, at times, driven children to make their faith decisions long before they were intellectually or emotionally prepared or fully aware of the implications of such decisions.

On the other hand, there are an increasing number of teenagers, as well as adults, who choose not to become church members at all, but rather prefer to be baptized into the church universal. They fail to see the logical and, in my opinion, biblical connection between baptism and membership in the local body of believers. In so doing, they may well be veering toward a quasi-Lutheran view of the invisible church. In short, how one understands the ordinance of baptism must be directly linked to one's understanding of the nature of the church. Many of the issues raised in the Reformation remain unresolved. And the less our people study and understand our history, the more likely they are to lose those perspectives which should be important to us as a believers' church today. Our forebears were avid students of the Scriptures. The observations they gleaned from Scriptures bear repeating today. It may well be that our youth will "buy into" our Christian heritage to the extent that adults show an appreciation for and understanding of that heritage. As we shall later demonstrate, it is the task of youth to become individuals, their own persons. This they must do for their own psychological and spiritual growth. It is therefore up to the adults to present them with the broader perspectives of the community of faith, our spiritual heritage, and our history. They want and need us to stand firm while they try out their wings. One way we can stand firm is by appreciating and owning our heritage.

The Separation of Baptism and Church Membership

One way to regard history is to note some of the ironies which emerge as the pendulum of time and attitudes swing from one extreme to the other. One of the ironies of church history is that many people who profess to be non-sacramentalist in fact are emotionally and practically much more oriented toward sacramentalism than they realize. What I mean by sacramentalism is that view of the sacraments (for Mennonites, "ordinances") which suggests that it is more than a sign or symbol and that something in the event itself actually transmits God's grace to the recipient of the sacrament. That is, it is a mechanism which releases God's grace. This is the traditional view of the sacraments held by the Catholics. Mennonites have said historically that the events of baptism and communion do not in themselves impart salvation or grace, but symbolize the prior and continuing grace which comes to the person who believes and makes a commitment of the will. But there are, in the believers' church, people who tend toward sacramentalism. This is the case in the two instances I noted earlier; of either pushing for an early baptism and church membership, or of not seeking church membership at all, just baptism.

In the former instance, the important thing is that the child experiences the sacrament of baptism, and thus becomes saved. Parents breath a sigh of relief once their child goes under the water and is baptized. The rite of baptism becomes the ultimate criterion to determine that the child is a member of the kingdom of God. This view does not take seriously the day-by-day growth aspects of church membership, choosing the Christian way and walking the path of discipleship. Such a view is not so ready to accept the ambiguities of life, that one can be on the way with Jesus without having arrived; or that the child, before the age of accountability, may be neither a saint nor a sinner. The child is simply *becoming*. And what the child becomes is dependent on a variety of factors, of which baptism is only one symbolic event.

Likewise, in seeking baptism without church membership, the mysterious element of the rite of baptism, characteristic of sacramentalism is emphasized. This stance assumes an ideal concept of the church and does not deal with the reality of a day-by-day encounter with brothers and sisters of like faith in the family of God. It is difficult to ascertain why the split between baptism and church membership occurs. In part, the trend has deep historical roots in Augustine's view of the two cities. It becomes simply a different slant on the meaning of the church/world dualism espoused at various times in history. And it is lodged in certain elements of the modern charismatic movement, particularly that aspect which does not wish to identify with any denomination. The Catholic charismatics, for example, have a built-in ecclesiology which prevails; but some other groups do not. All too often when the meaning of Christian commitment is spiritualized as strictly a matter of inner personal piety, there tends to develop a lack of appreciation for the church as a covenant community.

A second factor in the separation of baptism from church membership seems to be a function of how the adolescent sees life. Adolescents tend to divide the world between their own sense of idealism and the realities they see around them. This can be construed as a kind of adolescent "rebellion," or breaking free from the values and systems of their parents. In this case it is a more subtle challenge to parental authority, because it is so "spiritual" in nature. The child claims to have a better faith than that of the parents, a faith which can survive quite nicely without their church! This leaves the church with a peculiar challenge to face. Are we prepared to face the challenge without giving in to it? Or without creating a reactionary backlash? It has been said in recent years that there is a tendency for youth to swing with the rest of North America toward theological conservatism. Many of their parents grew up in the restless 60s when theological liberalism prevailed or at least influenced them. "Teenage rebellion" takes on a whole different meaning in that context! But it does not change the fact that parents today, like parents of every generation, are interested in their children, greatly concerned, and sometimes anxious and confused about how to relate to them. And parents who are part of the Mennonite Church today are concerned that their children may also find a meaningful place in the Mennonite Church.

The Challenge of Free Choice

The Mennonite Church holds as an ideal the individual decision for Christ and the church. In a sense, we expect a first-generation believers' church movement to emerge in each generation. But we are also part of a long history and tradition. How can we in each generation gain and regain the vitality of that first-generation freshness of Christian decision? We may have idealized our Anabaptist roots to the extent that we expect conversion in each generation to become a type of heroic individual decision, made consciously against the whole tide of worldly pressures from without, and quite apart from peer-group pressures within the community of faith. In this context we ask ourselves, what is the nature of Christian conversion and Christian commitment? Is it valid for youth as a group to decide to join the church? Does a group choice constitute the kind of individual and conscious decision which we feel the Bible teaches? Our ideals are confronted with certain realities. We expect our youth to have freedom of choice. But in reality "the cards are stacked" in favor of a decision for Christ and the church.

At best this decision, with sensitive nurturing of parents, pastors, and teachers, becomes a willing affirmation of a commitment to Christ as Lord and Savior and to his church, owning the best in our heritage of faith. At worst, the decision becomes a forced issue of parental and/or peer pressure to conform. In many cases, for all practical purposes, Mennonite baptismal classes are no different from the confirmation classes of other traditions in which youth at a given age almost automatically join the church. As an automatic process we would create less fuss, less ambivalence, and less anxiety if we would baptize infants! I do not recommend this course of action, but point this out to show how fine the line becomes between a sacramental and symbolic view of the rites of the church from a practical if not theological perspective. What I *am* saying is that we must be prepared to carry the challenge of our believers' church theology, view of baptism, and church membership to present the call clearly to each generation. C. W. Stewart, who did a developmental study of the religion of youth, has noted a "three-generation phenomenon." That is, if parents have a "firsthand" experience with faith their children will practice the faith, but for socially satisfying or conventional reasons. The grandchildren will either be indifferent or irreligious or again come into a "firsthand" experience.[1] This suggests that in each generation, we are only one generation removed from paganism, or nonbelief.

The question which should challenge members of the believers' church is this: If we still deem it to be a biblically sound practice to baptize adults upon their confession of faith as an outer sign of a prior decision, made of their own free will, do we have the courage to maintain that view consistently? In short, do we have the courage to be radically nonsacramentalist? What kind of Christian do we expect our children to become? If we expect their faith to be carbon copies of our own faith, we may as well take them to the altar as infants for baptism. If we really want them to be actively involved in deciding to be Christian, we have to be ready to let them go. A choice is no choice at all if there is only one option. We must be ready to let them choose freely. Each generation must decide the shape of its faith commitment.

We also hold this view of free choice in tension with our role as nurturing parents and a nurturing church. We do not always give our children free choice, especially when we feel they may be seriously harmed by the wrong choice. We do not place milk, water, whiskey, and poison before them as equal options. As we teach we weight the choices in favor of life, not destruction. So if we take our role seriously, I suspect that our children will become the kind of Christian that we as parents really expect and hope they will become. Have we today, in our concern to give children the freedom of choice in every aspect of their lives, not taken the church away from the family as a whole? Were not our Old Order Mennonite brothers and sisters right, in part, when they worried about what would happen when we leave Christian nurture in the hands of the specialists? In Ontario, we received a partial answer to these questions in a brief questionnaire distributed among pastors of the conference. The questions concerned practices regarding baptism and church membership studies in the congregation. One question asked concerned the context in which the baptismal candidates made their commitment of faith. The settings in which commitments were made, listed in rank order from highest to lowest, were home, membership classes, public meetings, small groups, Sunday school, camp, Mennonite Youth Fellowship. From this rather limited data, it appears that the home still plays an important role in the nurture and evangelism of children.

In this chapter, then, we have dealt with the question of how our youth will choose to follow Christ, become members of the church, and seek fellowship with believers in the Mennonite Church. We have recognized an implicit dilemma in the believers' church. If we really give our youth the freedom to choose we risk that they may not choose Christ at all. But if we allow them no choice, how have we retained the believers' church vision?

Chapter Two

Affirming Our Beliefs

I always knew that I was a Mennonite. It did not seem to make that much difference back in the hills of Erbsville where I came from. There I attended grade school with Roman Catholics and Lutherans, and valued one boy from each group as my two best friends. On Sundays I went to Sunday school, and had another set of friends. The two groups never met each other. Still, it did not seem to make all that much difference to me then. The various parts of my world fit together as a complete and usually happy whole.

Things changed a bit when I entered high school. In 1961 when I was fifteen, I had not heard about "the Anabaptist vision." But I was acutely aware of being part of a peculiar people, the Mennonites. And that made a lot of difference in my life. When I went to high school, I did not attend the school dances, "because Mennonites do not dance." I did not take part in army cadet training in the physical education classes, "because Mennonites are nonresistant." So during physical education classes, I sat alone in the corner of a study room for the duration of that part of the course. There

I began to ask myself, "What does it mean to be a Mennonite?" Because I did not dance, for the first time in my life I became aware that I was indeed a citizen of another world. I had a rather limited circle of high school friends. And again I asked myself, "Is that what being Mennonite is all about?" Perhaps that is when I first started to theologize in any self-conscious sense.

In the days of my childhood, my taste in theology was as nondiscriminating as my taste in music. I say this descriptively, not unkindly. I grew up listening to country gospel music, and no doubt absorbed a great deal of country gospel theology! And I sat under a variety of Sunday school teachers and preachers, most of whom were very much influenced by evangelicalism. In retrospect, though, I detected a certain amount of Methodism in one of them.

When I was seventeen, my friends and I went to church twice on Sunday and once in the middle of the week. We debated with our Sunday school teacher whether it was right to go swimming on Sunday. We discussed the pros and cons of the Revised Standard Version of the Bible. And we discussed whether it was right for our girl friends to cut their hair and not wear the prayer veiling. On these and similar issues, I cut my theological teeth. That year, Harold S. Bender came to Kitchener for the seventh assembly of the Mennonite World Conference. And we had a new pastor, fresh out of seminary, who spoke about "the Anabaptist vision." Although I did not grasp entirely what he was talking about, I knew it was supposed to make a great deal of difference in how I viewed my heritage of faith. Since then I have discovered that it makes a great deal of difference about a lot of my theological views. I too went to seminary, and came back and spoke of "the Anabaptist vision." In response I caught more than a few people yawning and upset some others. This story could be repeated many times. Only the people change, and perhaps some of the issues.

What Is the Nature of the Church?

The issue at stake in this discussion is the nature of the church. One cannot speak of one's understanding of the meaning of baptism and church membership without, in the same breath, betraying one's understanding of what the church is. The New Testament Greek word which best describes the church is "koinonia." It is best translated into English as "fellowship." "Community" as a term best designates that group which has fellowship. Thus the church may be described as "a fellowship community." In this community, as described in Acts, there is praise and prayer, eating together and communion, baptism and adding to the household of faith those who receive the gospel. There is caring and sharing as each gives generously to the common cause (Acts 2:41-47). In keeping with the biblical testimony, the Mennonite Church understands itself to be a *visible, believing community of faith*. We believe that the most visible manifestation of God is his calling together a believing community. This community experiences a new quality of life— Christian love and discipleship under the direction of the Holy Spirit. (For a more thorough study of the New Testament church, read *These Are My People,* by H. S. Bender.[2])

We believe, furthermore, that adult baptism is the appropriate symbol by which we indicate our willingness to identify with the people of God in this fellowship community. We make conscious choices and make them known before God and in the presence of the fellowship community. We hold that believers are baptized into the visible church, which has worldwide locations or fellowship groups. But in a practical sense our primary commitment is to the local congregation, where we can give and receive counsel and are nurtured in faith. It is also true that baptism identifies us with the church universal and that "cloud of witnesses" both present and past who have been faithful to Jesus Christ. That awareness encourages us to be faithful *where we are.* Therefore we believe that baptism is the event by which we covenant with God and each other to live the Christlike life. We are, as Paul suggests, raised with Christ to "walk in newness of life" (Romans 6:4). And to help bring about this quality of life, we need each other. At baptism, we also covenant to give and receive counsel in the congregation. We enter into covenant with the congregation in a process of discernment, admonishment, and moral solidarity—that is, we hold certain Christian values in common.

If baptism is the *covenant-making* event, the communion service is the *covenant renewal* event. In the act of communion, we remember what happened at the cross. We acknowledge our dependence on Christ and the sacrificial love which he displayed there. But we do not stop there. We acknowledge also that in that act Christ brought the church into being as an extension of his body. Thus the words "this is my body" extend to refer to the fellowship of believers.[3] Our Anabaptist forebears often said that the cross means little if it is not borne once again in the church, the body of Christ. That same self-giving love which drove Jesus to the cross must also motivate us in the church and in our relation to the world. When we eat and drink together, we renew our covenant of love and mutuality. Christ binds us together.

Another way to discern the meaning of communion is to ask "when is communion *not* communion?" As John H. Yoder has pointed out, in most traditions the answer lies in one of two directions: either the focus is upon the sacramental status of the officiating person (Is he or she properly ordained?), or upon the right doctrinal understanding of the meaning of the emblems. In 1527 at Schleitheim, some of our forebears suggested a different emphasis. For them the question of when communion is not communion had as its focus the participants. They said that communion is not communion when there is an absence of real community, solidarity, Christian love and fellowship among those present.[4] This view is borne out in 1 Corinthians 11 where Paul's concern is that we "rightly discern the body."

This brings us back to my story. It was the custom in our congregation to have a preparatory service the Sunday before communion. Considerable emphasis was placed on 1 Corinthians 11:27-29. I trembled lest I should eat and drink unworthily and thus drink damnation to my soul. I did not know then that the bread did not change its essence at communion. (Though the way it was cut and served had little resemblance to the bread which we ate at home for nourishment!) To further add to the awesome tone of communion, many of the ladies wore black on that day. Communion was taken in fear and trembling, not as a joyful celebration of the resurrected Lord! Little did I realize then that communion was not a sacramental event, such as we defined in chapter one. I remember the horror I felt at age 10 when a father in the same pew gave his restless child a bit of the communion bread to keep him quiet. Such sacrilege! Now I am certain that if people were asked about their understanding of communion, they would have seen it as a symbolic event and not mechanistic. But it seemed that their attitudes and the tone of the event belied that view and seemed more indicative of a sacramentalist view.

Let us reflect on the theological issue here. Admittedly, I have overstated the case to make my point. The diagram will help clarify what is meant by sacrament and symbol.

spiritualism	symbol/sign	sacramentalism
Society of Friends	Pentecostal, etc. Mennonite Baptist, etc. Methodist	Reformed Calvinist Lutheran Anglican Episcopalian Roman Catholic
description "the inner light"	*description:* "an outward sign of an inner faith" —a joyful celebration	*description:* "Absolute means of grace," actually conveys grace in a mysterious transfer as one receives the rites.
manifestation: —no rites —free church tradition —emphasis on discipleship as the "outer sign"	*manifestation:* adult baptism, free church tradition, conscious choice gifts of the Spirit (Pentecostal) —verbal testimony —Christian lifestyle (Baptist, Mennonite) —infant baptism, confirmation (Methodist)	*manifestation:* infant baptism —effect is remission of every sin, actual and original —folk religion and state church —passive recipients, later active confirmation

Any diagram or schematic representation will, of course, present a stereotype. We must recognize that the various categories in this diagram flow into each other. For example, some Methodists and Lutherans may be closer to each other then the diagram indicates; others may be considerably further apart. We should recognize also that today in most traditions, Catholic or Protestant, the sacraments or ordinances are seen as dramatic events with the purpose of serving as "faith prompters." There are no doubt various shades of understanding regarding whether the dramatic event itself does or does not actually impart grace in a mechanistic sense. For our purposes here, as it has been historically understood in our denomination, the issue is focused upon whether the participant in the sacraments, particularly baptism, is an *active* or a *passive* recipient. In traditional Catholic thought, a person becomes a living soul at conception and therefore is in need of salvation. Infants receive the sacrament of baptism passively, and through that act are saved. Godparents speak on their behalf, pending the later time when at confirmation the children "confirm" their willingness to be part of the covenant in the church. So a child, in need of salvation, may even be baptized before birth, "in the uterine waters."

At the other end of the polarity are the Friends (Quakers), who have no outward symbols, but rather speak only of the "inner light" which testifies to their faith. The only outward sign of one's faith should be one's deeds, the fruits of the Spirit which give outward testimony to one's status before God. Historically, Mennonites have stood between these polarities, affirming the value of outward symbols to signify an experience of the heart and will. What saves us is not the symbol, but our willingness to align our will with God's will in an act of faith. We have adopted the term "ordinances" to denote those practices which we feel Jesus "ordained" or invites us to participate in by his words or example. The term is also useful to distinguish what we mean by events or rites which in other traditions are called sacraments. The two main distinguishing features of our theology are: (1) that the recipient must be consciously aware of what is happening and chooses to be involved in the event, and (2) that the event is a symbolic event which may serve as a faith prompter by participation in the drama, but which has no mechanistic function in imparting grace or salvation. God's grace is given in the experience as a whole.

It calls for considerable perceptiveness and sometimes courage for Mennonites to take their stand on the sacrament-symbol polarity in the midst of a Christian history so dominated by mechanistic sacramentalist practice and thought. Historically, infant baptism is not the only point at which we encounter this sacramentalist practice. For centuries of Christian history, under Constantinianism, adults were baptized upon conversion from pagan religions. Their baptism was seen as being in itself sufficient for salvation but often their practices and beliefs did not change. So the church in many places consisted of baptized pagans. We are always faced with the danger of baptizing people on the assumption that they are Christians and place great emphasis on the baptism event itself as the ultimate indicator of whether or not they are part of the kingdom of God. That was the context out of which the Anabaptists of the sixteenth century spoke. It is not my intention here to review in detail the historical debate of adult versus infant baptism. Anabaptist studies show that even in the sixteenth century the issue of adult versus infant baptism was not at the outset the central concern of the Anabaptist movement. They would not have chosen to fight their Reformation battle on that front at all. Nevertheless, it become focused there. Their primary concern was for a clearer understanding of the biblical view of the church. Baptism became the focal point for that broader debate.

Dirk Philips in his *Hand Book* speaks lucidly and extensively on the nature of baptism, particularly in defense of adult baptism. Like Hubmaier, he begins with the Reformation cry of "faith alone" and explains briefly the process of salvation. We are saved by faith through the grace of Christ. That faith is worked in us by the Holy Spirit. From salvation comes love, and love leads to obedience. That obedience can only be to one master. Baptism is a sign of that salvation. Specifically, it signifies the believer's repentance or "death to the flesh" and "resurrection into that newness of life in Christ" and the fellowship of the body.[5] This view of salvation and the meaning of baptism is standard within the available Anabaptist writings. The Schleitheim article of faith states that baptism is for all who have been taught repentance, who truly believe their sins are taken away, who desire to walk in the resurrection of Jesus Christ, and who themselves desire it and request it. A cryptic note is added to the latter statement: "Hereby is excluded all infant baptism."

The key words, which were at the center of the defense of adult baptism, will remain at the center of our discussion. They are "know," "understand," "faith," and "right comprehension." Because infants do not comprehend the meaning of baptism, they should not be baptized. Great emphasis was placed on the Great Commission of Jesus, in which believers are exhorted to baptize and to teach. You cannot teach infants; therefore, you cannot baptize them. Philips insisted that, though children need to be taught in the Scriptures and moral living, nevertheless, the kingdom of heaven belongs to them without baptism. In short, children are not in need of baptism for salvation.[6] The Mennonite Church statement on "The Nurture and Evangelism of Children," adopted in 1955, states: "children, being covered by the atonement of Christ, are spiritually safe...."[7] To further argue in favor of adult baptism in Mennonite circles would, I suppose, be like bringing coals to Newcastle! If for purposes of dialogue with those who need to be convinced you need further evidence, you may wish to review the arguments in Rollin Armour's book *Anabaptist Baptism.*[8]

Given the basic ground rules such as "in Scripture alone" and "by faith alone," it is relatively easy to debate the issue of adult versus infant baptism. The issue becomes much less clear when one asks such practical questions as the following: "When is one an adult?" "How old is old enough when it comes to making a valid decision about faith?" "At what age is one accountable for sin?" These questions are being asked today. The Anabaptists asked them then, too. There was no consensus then on the matter of the age of maturity. While Menno Simons does not try to arrive at a specific age, he does insist that those being baptized be accountable. My reading in various sources reveals five criteria by which they attempted to clarify this matter:

1. Baptism as a sign of conversion and faith must be entered into with a conscious decision; therefore the *will* must be developed. Some thought that this happened at about age six or seven years.
2. Some said they must be old enough to, of their own accord, desire to hear the Word of God.
3. Some said they should be old enough at baptism "to have a fresh recollection of it all their lives" (Müntzer).
4. The "imitation of Christ" view suggested that thirty years would be a good age!

(a) Consistent with that, they said that original sin was not fully developed until thirty years of age.

(b) The example of Jesus tells us at least that it was a weighty matter, not to be entered lightly or at too young an age.

(c) At least, they said, we must be able to understand its meaning.

5. Some saw the Old Testament as suggesting that eighteen is the age of maturity and could be used as a pattern.

In any case, there did not seem to be much anxiety about what might happen to their children in the intervening years. Were they more certain of their own positive influence on their children than some of us? Or were they so engrossed in other issues that they had no time for worry? One father wrote to his "little daughter" from prison before his execution. He entreated her at great length to follow him in the faith, but always with the additional consideration— "when you attain to your understanding." A woman wrote to her eldest son: "to exhort you that you should begin to fear our dear Lord, for you are getting old enough to perceive what is good and evil." Further reading in *Martyrs Mirror* yields numerous references which reflect the youthfulness of some of the Anabaptist martyrs: "Two young girls," "a lad of fifteen years," "together with two young maidens," and "a young lad, named Rudolph Suhner, who, though young in years, was old in faith and knowledge of Jesus Christ." The latter reference speaks of a certain measure of maturity other than chronological age. Their commitment was such that they were prepared to die for their faith.[9]

Predictably, modern biblical scholarship is divided on the matter of infant vs. adult baptism. Largely this follows traditional denominational lines, but not always consistently so.

For example, Karl Barth, from the Reformed tradition, fails to see any explicit New Testament support for infant baptism. This still leaves open two possibilities. One is to say that infant baptism may still be *implied* in the New Testament. The other is to simply make tradition the norm and continue to practice infant baptism, the New Testament notwithstanding! We note that at least two eminent scholars, Joachim Jeremias and Oscar Cullmann, still maintain that infant baptism can be justified on the basis of the New Testament. One also reads of several Roman Catholic bishops who are practicing and advocating only adult baptism—one in New York State, and one in France. The Reformation is not over yet!

Youth Will Follow Our Affirmations

The concern in this chapter has been to review and affirm some of the core beliefs which our forebears held and which we still believe to be biblical today. Particularly, our beliefs about the nature of baptism, communion, and church membership are all linked to how we view the nature of the church. Mennonite youth will affirm these same or similar beliefs to the extent that we feel comfortable in owning them as our own. As a denomination we have been shaped by many theological forces, mostly from outside our circles. We have to develop a self-conscious discerning spirit. We must be open to new insights. We must also be aware of our own history. And in all things we must test the spirits to see that they are from God. The best way to do that is to do, as the Anabaptists did, a careful study of the Scriptures in the context of the discerning community of faith. If we give our youth the legacy of sound biblicism, they will learn to embrace sound theology as well.

Chapter Three

Growing to Maturity in the Church

People, made in the image of God, have the capacity to think and reflect on the meaning of life and their experience of life. This ability needs to be developed. We are not born full-grown physically, mentally, or spiritually. Paul was aware of this when he said, "When I was a child ... I thought like a child, I reasoned like a child ..." (1 Corinthians 13:11). In 1 Corinthians 14:20 he says, "Do not be children in your thinking; be babes in evil, but in thinking be mature." Obviously Paul was not thinking in psychological terms when he said this; for the practice of psychology as a "science" is a much more recent development. But Paul had keen insights into human nature. As he struggled within himself, he was aware of what Elizabeth O'Connor has dubbed "our many selves." Paul and other biblical writers call us to spiritual maturity. Jesus calls us to that "singleness of eye," that is, a clear sense of direction and purposefulness in life. The message of the gospel is that we can be whole persons, in body and mind. That is reflected in the healing ministry of Jesus, who healed the body and cast out demons (healed troubled minds). The life-giving principle of the gospel points toward what we can become, as mature spiritual beings.

Two basic issues will be the foci of this chapter: (1) What is the relationship of spiritual maturity to psychological maturity? (2) In what ways and to what extent can we use the social sciences to arrive at a meaningful understanding of faith questions? We must be aware that there is no one overall system of psychology with which we may compare our theological system or biblical understanding of the nature of humankind. Rather, there are various theories which one may apply, some more helpful than others. Not being a scholar in either field I cannot speak with authority on the relationship of psychology to theology. But in my studies and in my experience of life, I have begun to find some clues which I would like to share here.

It is apparent that "spiritual" and "psychological" questions have similar roots in the minds of people. Psychology as a field of study began in the thinking of philosophers attempting to discover the nature of humanity. Our understanding of where the emotions are seated has shifted in our anatomy! The Bible speaks of "bowels of compassion," regarding the emotions to be seated in the lower anatomy. Later thinkers identified feelings with the intellect. Today, in the generation of psychiatry and encounter groups, we are urged to freely express our "gut level feelings"! Through all of this, though, there is a sincere attempt to understand more fully who we are. It reflects an ongonig self-consciousness of humankind, our ability to reflect on the experiences of life. Some would suggest that we are progressively more sophisticated in our ability to understand ourselves. The suggestion is that we are more complex and of a higher order of human beings than more primitive societies. That may be debated by social scientists and historians. It is clear, certainly, that this may be debated biblically with regard to moral concerns. In any case, it is clear that as individuals we do develop in our ability to know ourselves and reflect on who and what we are.

Let me once again tell my story, a story with which many may identify, then pause to reflect on what it means. When I was five years old, I played in the sandbox. Hearing a humming noise, I looked up to see an object in the sky; my brother said it was an airplane. I was fascinated by the prospect of having that airplane as a toy in our sandbox. After all, it seemed to me to be about a foot long, just right for a toy! And I thought, perhaps if I had a real long ladder, I could climb up and reach out and bring it down. Also when I was five, as I lay in the grass beside the house and saw the clouds moving by, I was convinced that the house was falling over! And we recall the words of the boy in *The Ransom of Red Chief* who asked, "Is it true that the trees' moving makes the wind blow?" At that age, I had not developed a sense of perspective.

Again, when I was five, I heard Sunday school teachers talk about "giving your heart to Jesus," a rather frightening prospect to me, since I had not yet learned the meaning of "figurative speech"! Only later, in the course "The Psychology of Education," did I learn that in our childhood development we move from the age of concrete reasoning to the age of abstract reasoning, at about age seven or eight. (Some say as late as age 12). There is no arbitrarily fixed age, but it is nonetheless true that before a certain stage in one's development one cannot distinguish between cause and effect or put things into perspective.

It should be apparent then that the theological language which we use to address our children must at least recognize that factor in their development and growth. I do not know when I started to think of God as Spirit, or even vaguely comprehended the meaning of the term "spiritual" as opposed to "physical." But it became quite clear to me in my late teens and early twenties that one cannot say, "I understand mathematics, history, English . . . and God," all in the same breath. Somewhere between my sandbox days and my current self-understanding my understanding of the world around me has changed. So too has my faith and my theological understanding. I am convinced that a central part of God's creation is growth—physical, spiritual, and psychological. Serious Christians should try to understand their own growth through whatever tools are available.

Sigmund Freud, the founder of modern psychiatry, was in dialogue with a Reformed pastor, Otto Pfister. In the book *Psychoanalysis and Faith* we see their growing mutual awareness that psychoanalysis and religion do not have to work against each other. This is so because psychoanalysis is, in the final analysis, a *tool* not a philosophy. Unfortunately, as Paul C. Vitz has pointed out, too many people have treated psychology as a new religion, and have created the cult of self-worship. With this note of caution before us, I should like to proceed nevertheless to see what we may learn from psychology to help us better understand how to relate to the spiritual needs of our youth.

Psychologists such as Skinner and Locke suggest that people are basically creatures of instinct, reacting only to outside forces. The human being is seen as primarily a bundle of nerves which react when stimulated. There seems little possibility in that system of thought for people to consciously choose a direction in life. The emphasis is on the early childhood experiences which shape one's life. The child's mind is seen as a blank slate on which experience

43

writes. This tends to be a deterministic view of life. On that ground, I reject it as inconsistent with my Christian belief that the person in the image of God is free to choose and to change. This will have special significance for our later discussion of the nature of conversion.

Abraham Maslow, on the other hand, sees the person as a self-actualizing individual, choosing from within the appropriate responses to life and "writing his or her own life script." In a similar view, Carl Rogers wrote the book *On Becoming a Person*. They present a helpful corrective to the earlier determinism but, as so often is the case, may tend to overdo it in the opposite direction. This psychological school of thought, especially in its more popularized forms, tends toward extreme individualism, evident for example in Wayne Dwyer's *Pulling Your Own Strings* and in many other popularized psychological self-help books. The Christian corrective to this is to remind people that we really do need each other. Nevertheless, the important contribution of this psychological school is the assertion that we must take personal responsibility for our lives and feelings.

What this means in terms of our present study of youth is that we must find ways to help youth take charge of their own lives from being totally dependent children to becoming mature, thinking, and loving adults. Likewise, in terms of their Christian faith, they must make it their own. Biblically speaking, they must move from "milk" to "meat" in their experience of the Christian faith as Paul suggests in 1 Corinthians 3:2.

In the second chapter we raised the questions: "When is one an adult?" and "What is the age of accountability?" This is related to our Anabaptist insistence on baptizing only such persons who can make a conscious free choice and decision for Christ and the church. Now we are faced with the task of attempting to answer these questions with the help of the tool of psychology. How we define maturity shall be pursued less by a deterministic view of psychology than by the concepts of self-actualization or personhood in a dynamic sense. For this perspective, I am largely indebted to Gordon W. Allport's book *Becoming*. He perceives that psychology has made the mistake of looking for measurable specifics and drawing universal inferences from these. He feels that we need to look between the specifics at the process of becoming. For our purposes, that reminds us that we cannot arbitrarily set ages and stages, for example, when the age of accountability actually happens. The stages of development blend into each other. What happens as we move from one stage to another may in fact be the important thing to observe. In that process of becoming lie the possibilities of health and security, or emotional upset and mental illness.[10]

From Allport I glean two significant facts regarding the development of the child to healthy adulthood.

(1) The child is basically an unsocial being, and must be transformed into a social person, capable of taking his or her place in a complex society. The child moves from a strictly inner-oriented stance to a growing awareness of the "other" in his or her life. By implication then, the child will through this process later become aware also of the wholly "Other" or God.

(2) It is important that the child work out the potential split between the "tribe" and his or her own personal autonomy. That is, the child wants and needs the love and security of the family, but does not want to sacrifice his or her individuality for it. This is an acute process for the adolescent. The chart on page 46 illustrates the potential confusion.

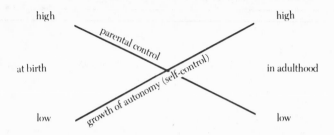

high   high

parental control

at birth   in adulthood

growth of autonomy (self-control)

low   low

It is clear that at birth, the child is totally dependent on the parents for survival. The child then grows in autonomy to the point of being totally independent and self-actualizing. Conversely, parental control decreases. Often by the end of their lives parents are as dependent on their children as their children once were on them. The point at which these lines of autonomy and authority intersect represents adolescence, in my schematic drawing. The lines of authority are unclear at this point. There is a dual ambivalence. At times adolescents wish to be very much on their own. At other times, they are all too happy to allow parents to take over the reins, for that seems to be more secure. By the same token, parents give intellectual assent to the belief that their child should begin to make his or her own way in life. But emotionally, they began to feel threatened that they are no longer an indispensable part of their child's life. How they *both* come out of that period in their lives is very important. In the best sense of the word, the youth has to "rebel," to really grow free and clarify his or her own identity and the lines of authority which he or she needs to claim. If this is true in the biological family, is it not equally true in the spiritual family, the church?

As I stated earlier, as Christians we do not believe that our direction in life is irreversible. There is always the possibility of change and growth and turning around (conversion). We recognize, however, that certain events in our lives or a certain environment will tend to predispose us toward certain choices, attitudes, and lifestyles. Erik Erikson in his work *Childhood and Society* has categorized eight stages along life's way.[11] He proposes that there are eight stages from birth to maturity, each having its own particular "box" from which one can emerge in a healthy or unhealthy direction. Though we do not see these as deterministic, it is helpful to note them here:

(1) In the first year, one can learn either basic *trust* or *mistrust* of one's environment. There is a basic need for security. This has later implications for the degree of trust one is able to place in people. It seems reasonable to assume that this could also extend to one's ability to trust in God.

(2) In stage two, at two to three years, there is a thrust toward *autonomy* which, if not positively rewarded, could as well turn to *shame or doubt*, a low self-image.

(3) *Initiative*, at ages four and five, could turn to *guilt*.

(4) *Industry*, at ages six to twelve years, if not rewarded, turns to *inferiority*.

(5) At the age of puberty and adolescence (12 to 18), the crucial issue is *identity* or *diffusion*. That is, the adolescent needs an integrated answer to the question "who am I?" He or she looks for these answers in terms of where they belong, in their cliques and peer group, and in their own sexual identity (what it means to be male or female).

(6) Erikson thinks that the healthy resolution of this identity stage will tend to determine one's ability to form healthy relationships. One is oriented to either *intimacy* or *isolation*. This occurs between ages 18 to 25, in "the marriagable years." Now the young adult sees himself or herself not only as a sexual being in relation to the peer group, but also to the larger society.

(7) Moving into adulthood, the person moves from *self-absorption* to *generativity*. That is, the adult becomes involved in a productive lifestyle, including also procreation, and learns not only to generate products and children, but also to care for what he or she produces.

(8) Finally, in the final years of one's life, one moves either to *integration* or *despair*. That is, one feels that one's life has meaning, that the various parts and stages of one's life have become a meaningful whole; or one yields to the despair that comes from a sense of worthlessness and futility.

Erickson's schema provides a way to describe a healthy mature person. When each of these critical stages in life is successfully negotiated and resolved, a mature person emerges. The mature adolescent, on his or her way to becoming a mature adult, has a good measure of basic trust, autonomy (self-reliance, inner motivation), initiative, industry, and a sense of personal identity; and is just beginning to experience intimacy. It has been suggested that the early years, up to age six, could be seen as a kind of "trial run" of one's later life. For example, it seems apparent that if one learns at an early age to basically feel secure and able to trust people (especially one's parents), one will later be better able to develop intimate relationships with others, including the possibility of the most intimate of all relationships, marriage.

In terms of Mennonite youth and church membership, the goal is to help our youth become productive, caring, loving church members. We need to nurture them through these other stages of life if we expect them to move toward this type of "generativity" (Erikson's term) rather than self-absorption. Our society places great emphasis on self-fulfillment, but it may be missing the mark of helping people grow to responsible maturity. Self-fulfillment is couched in

48

very individualistic terms, rather than in relational terms. So marriages have to be dissolved, if the individual does not feel "fulfilled as a person." Our society has perpetuated a type of ongoing adolescent stance to life, and we are reaping the results in people who are unable to sustain intimate relationships. There seems also to be a logical connection between this trend to self-absorption and the current inability of many to deal with authority. I think particularly of parents who are frustrated in rearing their youth. We need to find a way to describe authority that does not trigger visions of legalism or an "authoritarian" stance. One of the more helpful ways I have learned to speak of "authority" is to take the root meaning of the word. That suggests that the person has "authority" who cares for what he or she has "authored." It is a further dimension of Erikson's concept of "generativity." Of course, this does not mean that parents have authority over their children for life simply because the children they have "authored" belong to them! We shall discuss these concerns further in chapter five.

We have shown, using several psychological models, particularly that of Erikson, that there are describable stages of development in people, and that we have different important psychological "tasks" to do at each of them. This is described more thoroughly in John Drescher's book *Seven Things Children Need*, in chart form.[12] We have also implied that how each of these tasks is done will affect one's spiritual experience or development of faith. Now we must explore whether there are also stages of religious experience parallel to the developmental stages of life. Again, the appendix of Drescher's book is useful here. There is a significant diversity of thought on this matter, and we cannot hope to exhaustively and conclusively analyze relevant theories here. Rather, I shall suggest several approaches which I think are useful for our purposes and which in my opinion point us in appropriate directions.

Gordon Allport was one of the first predominant contemporary psychologists to attempt a systematic study of this in his book *The Individual and His Religion*. Though we may not agree with all of his conclusions, we may get some helpful clues to an understanding of the nature of the religious experience of children (infants) and youth (adolescents). He reminds us that the infant lacks the ability to think abstractly, and of course most things religious are abstract (God, values, theological ideas, etc.). Allport's inference from this is that what might be seen as "religious sentiment" in infants by those around them may in fact be simply a social response. The child may learn the rituals, but not their essential, abstract significance. If the child has any sense of God at all, it is God in the image of humankind. ("Anthropomorphic" is the word which describes this tendency.) The child's main concern is to belong in the family and in society.

It may be debated whether a child is so totally preoccupied with self as to not be able to become aware of others, and the "otherness" called God. Certainly it is not only children who have anthropomorphic views of God! This presents a real challenge to the church to present models for our children of godly living, what we usually call "Christlikeness." We need not, nor do we intend to, invalidate the significance of the child's religious experience simply because it is immature. But we need to clarify the nature of his or her experience. The child's religious experience must be affirmed for what it is—a desire to belong. This becomes the foundation for the child's later choices, to take ownership in Christ's church and to take his or her rightful place in the Christian community.

It is credible to suggest though that the type of religious experience of adolescents is qualitatively different from that of the preadolescent child. John Westerhoff III, Kohlberg, and others all agree, though they each formulate their own schematic portrayals of this fact. Allport maintains that true religious sentiment really only begins with puberty. That is a value judgment, which we may not necessarily accept. But his description of the religious experience of adolescence is helpful for our purposes. Allport holds that at puberty the adolescent becomes more fully aware of a fracturedness in life between the real and the ideal world. This is soon translated into terms of good and evil. The adolescent is very idealistic, often a moral absolutist, expressing harsh and positive moral judgments. In this period the adolescent takes ownership of religious attitudes which he or she had simply accepted as secondhand fittings from parents and others. (In Westerhoff's schema this is called "affiliative faith.") In the adolescent, the religious awareness overlaps with other sentiments. At puberty, love has its own peculiar awakening, and is often transposed into religious adoration. Reverence is often stirred by the beauty of nature. He or she seeks vivid experiences, and will attempt to recapture their inspiration. Such, for example, may be the case in the crisis experience of conversion. The adolescent will seek further similar experiences. The prayers of the adolescent may sound like love poetry to Jesus. [13]

The phenomenon of adolescence is one which our Western society has created, but has not well understood. In traditional societies, children move smoothly from childhood to adulthood, without much of the trauma associated with adolescence, punctuated only by the critical moment of the initiation rites. We have created the turbulence of adolescence. Have we also created with it a certain style of religious sentiment, such as Allport describes? For example, 95 percent of the reported crisis conversions have happened during the adolescent years. What is the relationship between these phenomena? Is conversion necessarily critical because of its essential nature, or is it a crisis experience because it happens during adolescence, which has its own built-in crises? These questions I find to be key to an understanding of conversion from the social-psychological perspective. We shall speak to this further in the next chapter.

Gideon Yoder in *The Nurture and Evangelism of Children* also acknowledges that there are observable differences in the nature of religious experience before and after the age of accountability, which he places at about twelve years. He draws the following conclusions concerning religious experience before the age of accountability:

(1) As late as twelve, the child thinks in concrete, not abstract terms.
(2) The religion of innocence is inherently beautiful, and is ignorant of evil, trusting, unsuspicious, receptive, docile, simple, and sincere.
(3) It is sporadic, because the child is unable to judge and to generalize.
(4) Though immature, the experience is one's religious foundation, significant for conversion and Christian growth.

Concerning the nature of religious experience after the age of accountability Yoder says:

(1) Descriptively, puberty itself is a kind of "rebirth." One might ask whether any rebirth is possible before puberty.
(2) At that point, the adolescent can begin to have a sense of history. That is consistent with the Old Testament view that the child *when he asks* is to be told the meaning of his history (Joshua 4:6).

52

(3) The young adolescent experiences a fracturedness or cleavage in his or her consciousness between reality and ideals.

(4) The function of conversion may be to once again convert this cleavage or splitness into an integrated and unified philosophy of life. Salvation, therefore, brings wholeness to the person who is aware of sin and separation from God and alienation.[14]

We have spoken a great deal of the progression of stages in human development. We would be remiss in not also recognizing that we could be described at any point along life's way as complex beings with various "systems" interacting to make up our self. This is usually spoken of as our "ego identity." One such model suggests that there are four main areas which make up the self: family relationships, vocation, sexuality and social relationships, and our value system. Each is linked to the others in a complex network. The interconnection is as important as each isolated factor. This model is relevant to our discussion of how Mennonite youth will relate to the church community. The problems between pastor and youth are often similar to those between parents and their teenagers. Given the fact of how deeply rooted our self-identity is in the family, we perhaps need to model our church life after family life. In so doing we can perhaps resolve both church and family issues together. This will be treated in greater length in chapter five.

We have described maturity in terms of developmental psychology and have drawn several inferences for the spiritual realm. The question may be raised whether we place an undue emphasis on intelligence as an attribute of psychological maturity. The danger here is that the dividing line for church membership would be between "thinkers" and "nonthinkers." But we know that relatively simple persons can have a deep and lasting faith. The intelligence factor is not necessarily a sign of maturity. Certainly it does not necessarily produce the ability to make commitments. There are those with great intelligence and high academic degrees who are unable to commit themselves to others in personal relationships, and who flit from one system of thought to the other without ever committing themselves to any one system of beliefs. They lack the singleness of heart that Jesus requires. So we must look to the *will* for manifestations of the kind of maturity required for Christian faith and commitment. The terms "will" and "heart" are synonymous in this discussion. When a person is able to turn from strictly self-centered interests to an awareness of the other in his or her life, that person is capable of making lifelong commitments. That is an act of the will, not necessarily related to intelligence.

Nevertheless, the two factors are not unrelated. There seems to be a certain minimum level of intelligence required before one can make autonomous and conscious decisions with lasting commitments as a result. This suggests that we need to involve persons with mental handicaps in the church on the same basis as we involve children—commensurate with their mental, psychological, and social development. They require a sense of belonging. Let us not expect more or less of them than they desire for themselves at the point of their development.

It should be apparent now that there are various stages in one's development and that certain theological truths can best be grasped at later stages in development. We need to recognize when the child's ability to reason moves from the stages of concrete reasoning to the abstract, as illustrated in the anecdotes at the beginning of this chapter. It is important to note carefully what the psychological agenda or task is for the person at a given age and tailor our teaching and nurture to that. We believe it is biblical that salvation speaks to the needs of the whole person—physical, mental, and spiritual. The assumption underlying this chapter, and indeed the whole book, is that we shall want to use all the tools at our disposal to better understand ourselves. These tools, when properly discerned, can also be listed among the gifts "for the upbuilding of the body of Christ" to produce mature Christian growth.

Chapter Four

Conscience and Conversion

When I was fourteen I developed an interest in hunting guns. Across the road from the school which I attended lived a man who had a rifle for sale. Without telling anyone, I saved the twenty dollars which he was asking for it and bought it. I carried it home from school that evening. Because I knew that mother would not approve, I wrapped it in a newspaper to take it upstairs to my bedroom secretly. Mother saw me on my way in the door and in her soft-spoken way called my name. "What have you got there?" she asked. I did not need her to tell me to know what I must do. I turned around and walked directly back to where I bought the rifle and got my money back. That may have been the longest mile I ever walked! But my feet felt considerably lighter on the way home. As I reflect on that incident today, I think it has all the essential ingredients of the Christian experience of guilt, grace, and the salvation which comes from conversion (turning around in my tracks). That is what this chapter is about.

What is "guilt" in psychological terms? The goal of life is

for the person to become an independent, self-actualizing person, responsible for his or her own actions. As a growing, independent young person, I made an autonomous decision to buy a rifle. Yet I obviously felt ambivalent about the wisdom of that act or I would not have tried to cover it up. I also chose, with a little parental nudge, to take responsibility for my actions. Both psychologically and theologically, people pay a high price for their freedom of choice. They establish a set of values (the religious person perceives them to be from God) to which they want to adhere. Their conscience ("super ego" in Freudian terms) makes this possible. But there is inner turmoil if their actions and their intentions do not coincide. That is what we call "conscience." "Guilt, doubt, and anxiety are the penalty people pay for having a conscience," says Gordon Allport in his book *Becoming.*[15] He makes some clear distinctions between two kinds of conscience. The conscience of the child he terms "opportunist." The conscience of a mature person he terms "generic." The former is typically infantile and simply functions in self-defense, to avoid punishment. It is a matter of personal expediency. The child soon learns to draw the connection between his or her actions and the possible consequences., The child's actions are always linked to the consequences, positive and negative reinforcements, not strictly to an inner motivation.

On the other hand, the generic conscience "reflects the growing conviction that a state of wholeness is possible even though we continually fight the battle between our impulsive nature and our ideals."[16] That is similar to what we see Paul describing within himself. "I do not understand my own actions. For I do not do what I want, but I do the very thing I hate" (Romans 7:15). The definitions of guilt then coincide with that of conscience. Infantile guilt is based on fear, shame, and doubt, and serves only to reinforce a low self-esteem. Mature guilt "is a poignant suffering, seldom reducible in an adult to a fear of or experience of punishment. It is rather *a sense of violated values*, a disgust of falling short of the ideal self-image."[17] Allport goes on to comment that there is no region of personality in which we find so many residues of childhood as in the religious attitudes of adults. In short, we have developed opportunist consciences by stating consequences such as "God will punish you for that," or "You will not get to heaven." Kohlberg makes the same basic distinctions, which he calls the "conventional level" and "principled level." However, he suggests that the conventional level occurs at age 11 or 12 to young adulthood. At that stage, the young person learns that conformity to parents and authorities will get approval, so the youth becomes a pleaser as a consequence. A bit later in adolescence, the younger person begins to understand the need for authority and rules, and begins to obey God's laws because they are good. The adult, who functions on the principled level, does what is right because of its intrinsic value. The adult internalizes divine laws so that they become his or her own. Whether we use Allport's terms or Kohlberg's, the point is the same: Mature conscience and mature faith go beyond the fear of punishment as a motivation for right living.

The opportunist conscience is most characteristic of primitive religions, with their system of taboos and the view that some mysterious forces will punish people's transgressions. A less primitive view, which is found in the Bible, particularly in the Old Testament, is the moralistic view of sin. In that view, sin is construed as departing from an external norm, in this case the laws of God. But the predominant thrust of the Bible, already emerging in the Old Testament and virtually

58

exclusively in the New Testament, is that sin must be seen in relational terms. As De Vries states: "The predominant conception of the nature of sin in the Bible is that of personal alienation from God."[18] This alienation results from self-love and rebellion against God (see Isaiah 53:6). The biblical writers had a keen sense of the tragedy of sin, not only because it was a transgression against some external norm of values, but because it was a conditon of dreadful estrangement from God, the sole source of well-being. Sin cut the person off from the source of all well-being. Salvation brought one once again in touch with that source. That is why the psalmist could say, "When I declared not my sin, my body wasted away" (Psalm 32:3). Jesus, too, recognized the intrinsic unity of the person in his or her physical, emotional, and spiritual dimensions, even in relation to the matter of guilt and grace. So he could say to a man, "Your sins are forgiven you" or "Rise, take up your bed and walk," and mean the same thing. It is a holistic view of life. And it is a holistic view of salvation.

The category of conscience which Allport terms "generic" and Kohlberg calls "principled" comes closer to the biblical view than the category "opportunist," though no doubt some refinements would be needed to make the categories say the same thing. The generic conscience is more typical of the one who is prepared to take personal responsibility for his or her actions. For purposes of our study, it seems appropriate to say that the development of the generic conscience and the age of accountability can be grouped together with freedom of personal choice. True, the child may choose to obey or not, and suffer the consequences. But true freedom of choice comes when the person chooses values without having to link them to reward and punishment alone. If I slap Rover often enough, he will quit messing up our flower beds. Does that make Rover a good dog? No, it simply makes Rover a well-trained dog. He still does not know or understand what is good or bad. He only knows what will result from certain behavior. I would not leave matters of judgment up to him! Likewise, I may have a son who never steals from the cookie jar. I may even classify him as "a good boy." But there are certain moral decisions which he is not yet capable of making. He is not mature enough to make them yet. Crude as the analogy may be, it indicates that there is a difference in the quality of moral behavior and conscience from the earlier to the later stages of development.

I shall not discuss in detail the age of accountability, which is traditionally a central focal point for discussion of the nurture and evangelism of children. This has been done by Gideon G. Yoder in a book by that name. The functional definition of the age of accountability is directly linked to the marks of maturity that we have already noted earlier. The age of accountability and the age of reason or moral consciousness are to be equated. The conclusion of this discussion is that one places the age of accountability in about the period 12 to 18 years, or at puberty. Yoder notes descriptively that puberty itself is a kind of rebirth. That is, a boy becomes a man, a girl becomes a woman. It has been demonstrated that the age of puberty is on the decline. Would that suggest too that the age of accountability may be placed at a lower age? That question needs further study.

It is in any case helpful to suggest that the age of puberty and the age of accountability are concurrent. One might ask whether any rebirth is possible before puberty. At puberty adolescents are acutely aware of that splitness in their consciousness between reality as they experience it and the ideals they hold. Then they become more fully aware of a sense of sin. This awareness of sin comes with the development of the awareness of the truly "Other." When children become aware of a sense of history and the larger world, they become aware also that not all is right in their world. This is consistent with the Deuteronomic suggestion that our children are to be told the meaning of their history. The questions the child asks are more than childish curiosity at this point. They arise out of a heartfelt sense that not all is right in the world, and particularly that not all is right in his or her world. The child then wishes to find a wholeness where there is such an acute fracturedness.

At this stage the adolescent becomes personally aware of the two great forces in the world, the forces of good and evil. When this awareness emerges, the adolescent is ready to look outside himself or herself to find wholeness. Conversion at this point is possible and is sought after. To convert one with this sense of fracturedness (sin) into a healthy person before God is the goal of Christian nurture and evangelism. But to attempt to make a child feel this sense of sin before he or she emotionally prepared for it is inappropriate and futile. It can only lead to an inordinate sense of guilt and shame which is not resolved. It is, in short, answering a question which the child is not yet asking!

We have been dealing in categories. But in keeping with my earlier assertion, we must remember that the person is always in fluctuation, in growth. We must therefore assume some fluidity between the categories we have noted. The child does not move from opportunist to generic conscience overnight. The child does not suddenly become accountable before God. Nor does the child suddenly become entirely aware of being a sinner—not unless we create a situation which forcefully convinces him or her of that fact. In the nurture and evangelism of children, given the understandings we have of personal development, we need to allow the child's understanding of God to grow, too. In summary, we should call children and adolescents at various stages of their lives to commit as much of themselves as they understand to as much of God and the Christian life as they understand. I am certain that God will honor that commitment, if we do.

We shall not attempt to define here whether a child as an infant is basically good or bad. The important thing to do is rather to realize that one is responsible for one's behavior when one is aware of consciously choosing it. Part of the function of childhood is to be self-centered, to develop a strong sense of personal identity. To label this as "sin" may be psychologically damaging. But self-centeredness, if it persists into adulthood, will create an unhappy and unhealthy existence, too. Then it may appropriately be labeled as sin, and dealt with. Self-centeredness is not sin until it becomes a conscious rebellion against God and self-seeking at the expense of others.

The Nature of Conversion

Having defined and clarified the nature of conscience, let us proceed with our discussion of conversion. In this process, we shall move back and forth between biblical-theological and social-psychological terms and categories. Sometimes the terms nicely coincide. Other times I shall define them to suit the context of this study for purposes of clarity and discussion. I hope we can get past the arbitrariness of categories to what they describe. The reader is reminded that in any case the categories of the social sciences are intended to be descriptive, not prescriptive. In the final analysis we shall take our pattern for life from the Scriptures, not from the social sciences. The purpose of studying conversion in this way is neither to diminish its importance, nor to detract from its Spirit-filled quality, but simply to describe it and better undertand it. My bottom line is that I affirm the need for conversion from sinful self to reorient my life to God.

In biblical terms, salvation from sin comes to the person who is ready to submit his or her life to God's rule, to put everything under the lordship of Christ. In theological terms this is conversion. It is turning away from self-centeredness and rebellion against God, and turning to God. It is accepting the fact that, though I acted in anger against God and went against his will, God is not angry with me. He loves me and reaches out in grace in Christ to invite me to be his child. A consequence of becoming God's child is that we pattern ourselves after Jesus, his Son. Conversion therefore also has results in the way we live. The experience of conversion brings wholeness to life. "The lost has been found" and "the blind now sees" are just two of many ways in which the Bible pictures this experience.

In psychological terms, William James describes conversion as follows:

> To be converted, to be regenerated, to receive grace, to experience religion, to gain an assurance, are so many phrases which denote the process, *gradual or sudden*, by which a self hitherto divided, and consciously wrong, inferior and unhappy becomes unified and consiously right, superior and happy, in consequence of its firmer hold upon religious realities."[19] (Emphasis mine.)

In his work *The Varieties of Religious Experience.* James shows two basic types of conversion. The moral-personal conversion is characterized by a struggle concerning personal sin and guilt and a yearning for personal redemption. This type is predominant among evangelicals and is considered to be the norm. The other type, ethical-social conversion, is characterized by despair concerning human injustice and yields a desire for greater love among people. A number of people report having both initial and subsequent experiences of spiritual awakening or conversion. The Harder-Kauffman study shows that "members who have had a *definite* conversion score significantly higher on the moral-personal type than members who have not."[20] We can with some degree of accuracy substitute "crisis" for the term "definite" above. From the results of this study we can infer that those who emphasize moral-personal conversion as described above also emphasize a crisis conversion experience. The terms may not be entirely synonymous, but may be used in a largely parallel sense, as I shall attempt to show.

Any category devised for purposes of the social sciences must of necessity be a stereotype. The term "crisis conversion" is certainly such a category. In sociological circles, it serves to describe what in theological circles is called "a new birth," a designation particularly characteristic of evangelicals in the revivalist stream. E. D. Starbuck and subsequently William James saw that the experience of conversion described thus "kept true to a preappointed type by instruction, appeal, and example. The particular form which they affect is the result of suggestion and imitation." James goes on to say: "In Catholic lands, for example, and in our own Episcopalian sects, no such anxiety and conviction of sin is usual as in sects that encourage revivals."[21] Starbuck, as cited by James, notes that in adolescence there is often considerable storm and stress. He goes on to suggest that theology builds on the tendencies of adolescence. "It sees that the essential thing in adolescent growth is bringing the person out of childhood into the new life of maturity and personal insight. It accordingly brings those means to bear *which will intensify the normal tendencies"* (emphasis mine). He notes that the emotional impact of "conviction of sin" is very similar to much of what the adolescent experiences in the process of maturation, including for example loss of sleep and appetite. He concludes that "the essential distinction appears to be that conversion intensifies but shortens the period by bringing the person to a definite crisis."[22] That is how "the new birth" experience looks through the eyes of Starbuck and James.

If the sociological category "crisis conversion" seems to be a stereotype, it may be that the experience which it describes has also been stereotyped in evangelical revivalism, and to a perhaps lesser extent in the Mennonite Church of the past several decades. The term "crisis" means primarily a crucial turning point, hence a critical moment. The Greek root itself means "a point of decision," and the verb means "to decide." It appears, however, that the sociological category uses the term "crisis" also with its secondary suggestion of strong emotional upheaval. It is unclear whether Harder and Kauffman's use of the term retains both the primary and secondary meanings. In any case, I shall use it in the context of my work in both senses.

Let me hasten to clarify then what we shall do with this term if we as Mennonites want to affirm the importance of the new birth. We have on the whole used the term "the new birth" from the beginnings of our denomination to today. Menno Simons used it and described it thus:

The new birth consists, verily, not in water nor in words; but it is the heavenly, living, and quickening power of God in our hearts, which comes from God, and which by the preaching of the divine Word, if we accept it by faith, quickens, renews, pierces, and converts our hearts, so that we are changed and converted from unbelief unto faith, from unrighteousness into righteousness, from evil into good, from carnality into spirituality, from the earthly into the heavenly, from the wicked nature of Adam into the good nature of Jesus Christ.   .

J. C. Wenger, who cites the above-quoted words of Simons, comments on repentance as related to conversion. He says it "has at least three aspects: intellectual, emotional, and volitional."[23] Nonetheless, as Mennonites we tend on the whole to avoid placing great stress on the emotional aspects of conversion and place more emphasis on it as a critical turning point. The crisis of the new birth in that sense denotes a significant change in one's life stance, with a keen awareness of making a conscious shift in direction at that critical moment and receiving renewal from God.

We have on the whole suggested that the new birth is not in itself an emotional experience, but that one feels the emotions linked to the upheaval of such a radical change of orientation from an old life to a new life in Christ. The emotions which accompany the experience may be positive or negative, happy or sad. The emotions are at best the by-products of the experience, not the experience itself. And we have been rather critical of emotionality for its own sake in the experience of conversion. We have also observed that some persons seem to need crisis experiences to grow spiritually (I use the term "crisis" now with its emotional connotations, too), whereas for others the waters run more smoothly as they grow in faith. We have in any case always said that real spiritual growth is solidified, not by the emotionality of the crisis, but by our conscious decisions made at that critical moment. Nevertheless, the emotional impact has been a large variable, depending on the settings and personalities involved. Therefore, I propose that "conscious decision" would be a more useful term than "crisis conversion" to describe what the Mennonite Church thinks of repentance and conversion. Through conscious decision a person is open to God's gift of the new birth, new life in Christ.

It is difficult to precisely correlate theological terms with the terms of the social sciences. For purposes of this study, I propose to use the term "crisis conversion" in a descriptive sense, with the emphasis on the decisiveness of the experience and on the emotional impact which accompanies it. Furthermore, I propose to use the term in a limited sense to parallel the theological term "the new birth." Even as I do this, I recognize that not all who use the term "the new birth" wish it to connote an emotional experience. The emotional impact is a considerable variable. Yet we can assume that some aspects of this variable must have been present in the New Testament story from which the term is derived. I refer of course to the story of Nicodemus' encounter with Jesus one night (John 3). The very fact that Nicodemus felt compelled to meet Jesus secretly already suggests that a certain degree of emotional trauma must have been present in the event. Consider what a radical break from the norms of his society and Jewish faith this must have been. If Nicodemus was in fact converted by Jesus that night, it seems that it must have been a crisis conversion experience. Likewise, even a cursory analysis of the conversion of Saul on the road to Damascus reveals that it was so traumatic that he was struck blind for several days. "Crisis conversion" and "the new birth" are, I believe, parallel terms from the social sciences and religion which adequately describe these two instances at least.

The question which remains, however, is whether the examples of Nicodemus and Paul are to be seen as normative prescriptions for the conversion of persons into the

Christian faith today. These are but two of various examples in the New Testament of people who encountered Christ and experienced salvation. The Bible clearly shows that salvation came to various people in various ways, according to their needs. Nicodemus was told that he needed to be "born again," or "born from above." The blind man received his sight, and with it new spiritual insight came. In fact, in Mark's account, the blind man needed a second touch. That suggests that we need to keep on making decisions and gaining new insights into our relationship to the kingdom of God through Christ.

Some Scriptures see people as enslaved to sin and so for them salvation comes as "redemption." Some are crippled and ineffective as persons and for them salvation comes as wholeness and healing. The Scriptures describe salvation in many ways. Theologians have categorized Scriptures into a systematic way of talking about salvation and conversion. The categories are useful for this purpose, but we must never let them overshadow the original saving acts of God in Christ which they are meant to describe. It seems plausible that if Jesus and the biblical writers had had access to psychological terminology, they might have used it also as one way to describe salvation and conversion. In any case, it is useful to employ the terminology of the social sciences in a strictly descriptive sense today in an attempt to better understand our experience of conversion and salvation.

Based on these definitions, the question should be raised as to whether everyone needs to experience a crisis conversion. Or in other words, does everyone's conversion need to be of the "born again" crisis variety? The question emerges in situations in which people somehow have always known that they are a part of the family of God. They have never experienced a singular momentous event of commitment or rebirth that they could point to; yet they are convinced that they are Christians. Does conversion then have more than one kind of manifestation? And are there different kinds of conversion, equally valid, for different kinds of people? Let us explore these questions, in order to better understand the nature of the conversion experience.

Let us briefly, from a Freudian psychoanalytic point of view, evaluate the assumption made in some Christian circles that everyone needs to experience a crisis type of conversion as an adolescent or adult. From that psychological point of view, a great deal hinges on how one resolves one's developmental tasks in the critical years between the ages of four to seven. At that age, a boy can either retain precocious ideas about being his own authority in relation to his father, or he can surrender from the position of usurper to that of the obedient child. Likewise, the daughter can either try to take her mother's place in the affections of the father, or she can surrender that status to her mother and become an obedient child. Many refinements of this schema could and should be made, especially in light of current concerns about sexuality and male-female roles. For our purposes here we shall take a more broad sweep of the Freudian material. The "surrender" of the child, as opposed to the "usurper" stance, could be seen as the psychological equivalent to conversion. It may have implications for how we relate to God, our heavenly Father. If that psychological task is not completed at that early stage, the child develops a kind of neurosis (mental illness) which later needs to be healed.

The adult sinner, in Freud's descriptive terms, could thus be one who did not grow healthily from his "once born" childhood. That person therefore needs to experience a radical shift or, to use the theological term, needs to be "born again." (William James coins the terms "once born" and "twice born.") When this happens in this later stage in life, it is a relatively abrupt change and may therefore be classed as a crisis conversion experience. In this case we need to emphasize that aspect of the crisis conversion experience which I had earlier relegated to a secondary place, namely, the emotional aspects of the experience. Why is conversion so traumatic for some people? Theologically, we have said this is because of their great sense of grief and guilt as they recognize the sin in their lives. In psychological terms, the trauma of this recognition is heightened in those who did not satisfactorily negotiate the psychological tasks that are to be done between ages 4 and 7. This will have considerable impact on the nature of their religious experience. Adult conversion, in this person's experience, becomes in both a spiritual and psychological sense the healing of a "sick soul" (William James' term). Remember again that Jesus sometimes spoke of healing persons and forgiving sins as part of the same experience. What remarkable psychological insight.

Later, Eric Erickson refined and revamped Freudian thought into his own schematic understanding of human development. In his model, the years 1 to 6 constitute a type of "trial run" of the issues to be dealt with more consciously in later years. The critical issue of usurper or obedience in the young child will emerge again in adolescence. There is, however, a relatively tranquil period of growth and learning which takes place between ages 7 and adolescence. There are therefore two critical periods in personal development; early childhood, and adolescence. How one resolves the early crisis will have significant impact on how critical the latter stage will be. And I use the term "critical" here also in the sense of emotional and traumatic.

The question before us is not whether everyone needs to be converted. The question is: What is the nature of conversion? How must we experience it? Must it be a crisis experience in order for it to be a real experience? To answer yes would suggest that the more critical it is, the more real it is, which surely is not so in fact. From our psychoanalytic analysis we have discovered that some souls, because of the healthy environment and sound nurture of family and church in their early formative years, do not experience that persistent "sickness" into adolescence. They seemingly need no basic abrupt or critical change—they need only to grow and become mature as children of their human parents and as children of the heavenly Father. For some, this growth is so uneventful that they can hardly pinpoint just when they became Christians.

When Jesus said to Nicodemus that he must be born again, was he saying that he must become a child again? In Freudian terms, was Jesus saying that Nicodemus must relive what he should have experienced in early childhood, but did not? For Nicodemus, at least, conversion was a critical experience in every sense of the word. For him, conversion meant a decision to yield to the authority of Christ. This yielding is surrender and submission of the will, but it is not simply knuckling under to a kind of regimentation. Nor, on the other hand, are we to be self-seekingly independent. Rather, there is an appropriate interdependence. Large spheres of conduct are left up to us, because God has given us the ability to choose. As we choose to follow Christ, we own our place as sons and daughters of God, "with whom he is well pleased."

The point of introducing psychological analysis here is also to show that mental health and the conversion experience belong in the same discussion, if we understand salvation in a holistic way. I am not suggesting that children at age 4 to 7 experience conversion in any theologically valid sense of the word. What I am saying is that what happens to children psychologically at that stage will tend to *predispose* them to certain varieties of religious experience in their later adolescent and adult years. The issue which we have addressed is why the decision to follow Christ can be a conscious yet very quiet event for some, while for others it may have a great deal of emotion involved. One answer which seems credible lies in the Freudian analysis we have presented. The analogy might be drawn like this: If sin is a spiritual sickness needing healing, for some people good basic nursing care and nutrition will do the job, whereas others need radical surgery. The end result is the same: the healing of persons under the skillful hands of the Master Healer. And so we have allowed psychology to inform us in a descriptive sense. In the final analysis as Christians we take our prescription for salvation from Scripture itself, in its testimony to the saving acts of God in Christ.

As pastors, teachers, parents and others in the church who work with youth, we must always adjust our preaching and teaching to the needs of the people with whom we work. It is helpful and brings a sense of relief to people to realize that there is indeed a *variety* of religious experience and that we are not cut out of the same mold. In psychological as well as theological terms, it is clear that we are still faced with the need for conversion, but here is opened the possibility that not everyone will experience it as a crisis event because for some much of the trauma is resolved early in life. That does not suggest that the person does not need to continue later in life to make conscious decisions for Christ. It is simply a credible explanation of what we understand the experience of conversion to be for some people—a quiet, healthy growth into Christian faith and maturity. It is also very much in keeping with the thrust of our historical faith that the Christian life is a life of discipleship and a walk with Jesus on the Christian way.

Having said this, what shall we do then with "the altar call" as a context in which people are brought to experience conversion? We have recognized for some years now that many people grow into faith without the critical experience of that staged event. For this, and other reasons, the Mennonite Church in many places has done away with the revival meetings and altar calls. But there may be many in our midst who in adolescent or later years need the crisis experience of being born again. Many may need it to be a cathartic emotion-filled experience such as the altar call once provided. The church may need to once again provide a context *in which those who need to* can experience in a dramatic and vivid way what it means to take a stand for Christ and experience the crisis of conversion as a turning point in their lives. Is it natural for us to put the kingdom of God first in our lives? If not, we should not be surprised if taking that stand creates a crisis of struggle and turmoil—perhaps more in some than in others. We are all constantly faced with decisions, if we are going to remain faithful and continue on the way with Jesus. We need to find ways to express these decisions and make them more vivid if necessary.

In my conclusion, on the matter of conversion in the adolescent religious experience I suggest the following:

(1) That adolescence (at or about the age of puberty) is a significant age for religious experience. It has also been shown, according to the Harder-Kauffman study, that the crisis type of conversion has been a large part of adolescent religious experience in the Mennonite Church in recent decades. However, a more recent study done by the Faith

and Life Committee in the Mennonite Conference of Ontario shows that the majority of adolescent decisions are made in the nurture contexts of home and church membership classes. One can infer from this that the nature of the decision is often not a crisis event.

(2) That adolescence is also the age of accountability is quite widely believed and is credible.

(3) There are various opinions concerning which age in the child's development is most crucial to growth toward healthy maturity. In any case it seems that for some people adolescence is critical. For them, a crisis type of conversion experience is consistent with the rest of the development. We could thus respond in one of two ways. We could capitalize on it and encourage a critical religious conversion in proportion to this critical stage in the life of the adolescent. Or we could work toward abolishing or diminishing the critical nature of conversion, so that it is not added to the rest of the adolescent's sometimes traumatic experience. The latter option would suggest that we should work toward diminishing the turmoil often associated with adolescence. Would there be merit in postponing conversion, baptism, and church membership to the post-adolescent years when the youth is more emotionally settled? However, we need to take seriously our belief that faith speaks to all of life's needs and should surely also be a part of the adolescent experience. We should rather concentrate our efforts on minimizing the critical aspects of adolescent development, with all the best resources available to us in our families and congregations. At that time, when development is rapid in all areas of life, it is not right to leave the adolescent to flounder alone.

(4) By insisting on a certain level of maturity before baptism and church membership, we need to address the question of how the children fit into the life of the church. We

74

will expand on this question in the next chapter. But in summary, in rejecting infant baptism we have missed its positive dimension: the way in which it demonstrates a sense of belonging to the family of God, the church.

(5) If we wish to minimize the crisis of adolescence, we should no longer expect highly emotional crisis conversion events, or at least stop acting as though they are the norm for everyone. That might suggest, for example, that we do not "stage" an event to drive youth emotionally to such an experience. Of course, this means that we must conversely increase our emphasis on nurture and recognize that children can *grow into faith* as well as *grow in faith.*

(6) In any case, the person who is mature is the person who owns his or her faith experience. Even in this more gradual sense of spiritual awakening the individual must consciously choose to be and continue to be "on the way with Jesus." Psychologically speaking, the person who does not take responsibility for his or her own life is not healthy. Biblically and theologically, the Christian must be a Christian by choice and is constantly called to make choices along life's way.

(7) It has been largely attested that those from outside the Christian faith have highly significant experiences of conversion and that they tend to take their Christian faith more seriously than those who have always been within the household of faith. For such people, a crisis conversion experience may be valid and desirable, for they can truly say, "Once I was lost, but now I am found." Those who grow up in a Christian home and congregation may not be lost in that way, yet they need to grow and make decisions too.

In this chapter we have explained the nature of conscience and conversion in the context of our understanding of human development described in chapter three. We have affirmed the need for all persons to consciously commit themselves to Christ and his church. But we have allowed considerable leeway for a variety of religious experiences, with their implications for the conversion experience. We only need to read the Bible again to discover the various ways in which Jesus met the many needs of the people. Above all, we seek wholeness and salvation for ourselves and for our children and youth in the church.

Chapter Five

Belonging to the Family of God

And stretching out his hand toward his disciples, he said, "Here are my mother and my brothers! For whoever does the will of my Father in heaven is my brother, and sister, and mother."
—*Matthew 12:49, 50*

See what love the Father has given us, that we should be called children of God; and so we are.
—*1 John 3:1*

We may speak of the church as "the family of God," from three points of view. First, from the biblical point of view. In the Bible, God is called our heavenly Father and Jesus encourages us to address him that way. Jesus refers to his disciples as his family. Paul describes us as sons and daughters by adoption. The Bible views the church as a dynamic, growing organism rather than a static institution. The family of God figure of speech is consistent with the New Testament view of the nature of the church as portrayed in Acts. The church, like a healthy family, is made up of people who share a common life and who care for each other. It is true also that the Christian faith is portrayed as a family affair in

77

the Bible. Several times in the New Testament reference is made to persons who were received into the Christian fellowship, "they and their house." Other times the church itself is called "the household of faith."

Second, the image of the family of God has good historical roots, too, in the Anabaptist-Mennonite tradition. Our forebears saw the dangers of institutional church forms. Hierarchy and power positions led to corruption and a spiritless church. But they were not satisfied with some of the more individualistic alternatives which the Reformers seemed to present. In the sixteenth century, therefore, the idea of the church as a believing community was recaptured and expressed in word and deed. This was based on their reading of the New Testament and the church portrayed in it. They saw the church as a brotherhood. Today we reshape the word so that there is no doubt that "sisters" are also included in this designation. "The people of God" captures the same essential meaning. So, too, does the term "the family of God."

Finally, in sociological terms it is a helpful analogy to compare the spiritual family to the biological family. It is helpful because it speaks to the relational and developmental questions of children growing up in the church and taking their place in the fellowship of believers. It is necessary to see the relationship of the family to the church because one interplays with the other to such an extent that it is difficult to ascertain which most shape one's life and values. It is a useful analogy also because both in family life and in the church there are two kinds of involvement— voluntary covenant commitments, and involuntary and relatively unconscious involvement. That is to say, everyone is in a family, but not everyone chooses to get married and form that kind of covenant. Furthermore, though everyone is

78

born into a family, not everyone assumes the same degree of responsibility and role in the family. Likewise, all who are in the church belong to the church, but not everyone chooses consciously to be part of the covenant. More on this analogy later.

Perhaps another personal anecdote will help to explain the focus of this chapter. When I was a teenager my closest friends were from my home congregation. Some of them were in fact also my cousins. Much of my life revolved around our congregation, particularly in relation to these close friends within the congregation. We learned together in Sunday school, we sat together in worship services, and we went to each other's homes for dinner after church. In the evening we went to church together again. After church we parked our various vehicles in the church parking lot and climbed into one car to go bowling or eat a pizza. It was not at all unusual for us to arrive back at the church parking lot by midnight and spend several hours in the car talking after that. Often our discussion focused on topics of great concern to us as teenagers, anything ranging from tractors to sex to faith questions, and not necessarily in that order! I look back on those years with fondness. They were my most formative years, particularly in regard to my faith.

I think it is more than nostalgia to suggest that there is a lasting benefit to living in a relatively homogenous society, including a constant interplay of church and the extended family. To live, work, play, and worship with a certain core group of persons produces a sense of security, wholeness, and general well-being. It gives substance in the broadest sense to the salvation which one experiences in the household of faith, salvation that speaks to all of life. The family and the church must continue to work together. The church remains the only institution in our society which ministers to people over their lifetime, from the cradle to the grave. In secure homes, in the supportive context of the community of faith, we shall be able to endow our children with a deep and lasting faith.

Having made these affirmations, biblically, historically, and from personal experience, it seems paradoxical that we need to ask the question, "What is the place of youth in the church?" The question is raised in the context of our view of the nature of the church. We believe that the church is to be made up of persons who have committed their lives to Christ and who have covenanted together to be part of a community of discernment, counsel, mission, and worship. This kind of commitment calls for mature persons. It is not kid stuff! Yet we feel that children are a part of the family of God. And we believe that they are safe in the realm of God's grace. It is indeed a paradox. They are in the church, but they are not the church. They are part of a community of faith which they have not chosen. So we need to understand and clarify where children and youth are to stand in the life of the church. They want to know, and we owe them a consistent explanation.

Let us renew some historical-theological background before answering the questions. Because much of the Christian faith has its roots in Judaism, it seems logical that we should look there to see if there is anything instructive for our purposes. There are two rituals in Judaism which have been seen as prototypes of Christian baptism. Beasley-Murray points out that there is in Judaism a rite of baptism roughly equivalent to the meaning of Christian baptism, linked to adult converts entering the Jewish faith.[24] Evidence suggests, however, that the real rite for entry into the Jewish faith is that of circumcision. Baptism with water came seven days later and was really a ritual cleansing or washing, to make the person fit for participation in worship. The Talmud suggests that the real "new birth" experience came from the circumcision rites. Baptism was primarily for cleansing, not for membership in the covenant community. Baptism was not seen as a mechanistic ritual which made a heathen into a Jew. It simply indicated the member's new stance as a ritually clean person in the community of faith. What may have confused the issue then, and of course later in Christian baptism, was that the vows which the convert learned previously were repeated in the baptismal rite itself, leaving it open to the suggestion that the acts and the words combined had a special power. Nevertheless, we cannot from Jewish practice ascertain that baptism and church membership are separate events, since they are so closely linked in the same sequence of events. The primary meaning of baptism in Judaism then was to indicate the ritual cleansing of adult converts in preparation to enter the worship life of the community. John the Baptist added to that concept the matter of radical conversion through repentance as the only way to be ready for the coming of the kingdom of God. It seems that his concern was to go beyond ritual cleanliness to moral cleanliness. That idea is picked up later by Paul in his description of baptism as indicating one's intention to "walk in newness of life" (Romans 6:4).

The other ritual in Judaism which may be instructive for our purposes is circumcision. Circumcision marked the initiation of Jewish males into the tribe or nation, the people of God. This was practiced on the eighth day after birth. Genesis 17:11 states: "You shall be circumcised in the flesh of your foreskins, and it shall be a sign of the covenant between me and you." In every respect, this ritual had the same effect as infant baptism does in those churches in which it is practiced today. In like fashion, in Hebrew practice, there is a "confirmation" event, the Bar Mitzvah. It means literally "son of the commandment." "Bat Mitzvah" means "daughter of the commandment." This basically indicates that the boy or girl has attained to both religious and legal maturity. For boys, this occurs at thirteen years plus a day. For girls, it occurs one year sooner. We see in this that long before the social sciences were developed, the Jews understood that girls tended to develop to maturity more rapidly than boys, at puberty.

It seems to me that the really instructive Jewish practice for us here is neither proselyte baptism nor circumcision, but the practice of Bar Mitzvah. At the time of Bar Mitzvah, the candidate is required to fulfill all the commandments. In theory, at least, he becomes a fully responsible person. There is some evidence though that this full religious and legal responsibility does not appear as part of the meaning of the event until the fifteenth century AD. And we must remember too that Bat Mitzvah (for girls) did not appear on the scene until the nineteenth century.

Bar Mitzvah seems to be a more thoroughgoing rite of initiation than our practice of adolescent baptism, in that it makes the person a full-fledged member of the community of faith in every respect. It implies that he has reached the age of physical maturity. At this age young people are thought to be able to control their desires. After this event, their vows are considered to be valid. Until thirteen, a son receives the merits of his father and is also liable to suffer for his parents' sin. After that, each one bears his own sin. "Blessed is He who has now freed me from the responsibility of this one" is the prayer of the Jewish father at his son's Bar Mitzvah.[25] This indicates a healthy attitude, a conscious effort on the part of the parent to help his child grow free and become responsible. In effect, it does not perpetuate adolescent needs to rebel to grow free. Nor does it perpetuate perennial adolescence. It is significant to note that in more recent years in certain Reformed Jewish congregations in Germany, confirmation was instituted in addition to Bar Mitzvah. They felt that at age twelve or thirteen the child did not understand the full implications of the ritual, so they confirmed its meaning at age sixteen or seventeen, upon graduation from secondary school. This fact should also be considered when we consider the question of when our youth may be deemed ready to take full responsibility in the covenant community of faith.

The above observations of Jewish practice have shown us a way to encourage mature Christian faith in our youth and to symbolize their willingness to accept the faith as their own when they have reached a certain level of physical and psychological maturity. It clearly portrays a minimum standard of maturity for active involvement and ownership in the covenant of faith (age 12 or older). But what shall we make of the idea that the circumcision of the infant marks him out as being part of the covenant community? No doubt the answer which comes most readily to us is that it is a form of "baby or child dedication," which we practice too, without the symbol of circumcision. In that sense, it is an encouragement to parents to nurture their children in the faith until such time as they can confirm their own intentions in that regard.

Practically speaking, the practices of circumcision, infant baptism, and baby dedication seem similar. Theologically speaking, there are significant differences. The first two suggest that in effect the child becomes a part of the covenant through the covenant commitments of the parents, "by proxy," so to speak. In the believers' church tradition, we believe that the event is really a parental dedication or commitment, and that the child does not at that point become part of the covenant agreement. However, the child is as much part of the covenant community from birth as a part of the family, not by choice, but by circumstances. What the child makes of these circumstances will depend finally on him or her, but in the meantime the choices will be shaped and bent in that direction by the nurture of the parents and the church, the family of God.

I agree with Vernard Eller's assessment that adult baptism is the covenant-making event for the individual and that communion is the covenant-renewal event. What happens when we transpose this idea back into Judaism and the Passover event? We do not see young children excluded from the Seder (the family passover meal), as we exclude our children from communion. In fact, to the contrary, the youngest Jewish child is at the center of the activity, asking the questions which the father then answers. Yet the child has not been confirmed as a member of the covenant. If the Seder is at all parallel to Christian communion, then we appear to be using communion in a more exclusive sense.

I raise this fact only because in certain circles in the Mennonite Church today, there are those who would argue that all children, baptized or not, belong in the communion event as participants. Personally, I am not very comfortable with that practice. The argument from Jewish practice breaks down at the point of the meaning of circumcision itself, from which event the child is seen as a member of the covenant people. Furthermore, Jesus' own words at the Last Supper suggest a significant break between the old covenant and the new, as exemplified in his own person. In the final analysis, we must model our idea of the covenant after Jesus' teachings. His call to discipleship is clearly a call to which mature persons can best respond. In my opinion, historical theology and the Bible both present ample evidence that this stance is credible and desirable, that is, that children would not be included in the covenant rites of baptism and communion.

From a social-psychological and developmental point of view, the strongest argument for infant baptism is the concept of family solidarity, the corporate community of faith as reflected in the phrase "you and your house." This lends unity and integration to the life of the young person. It may be argued that the child who has been baptized as an infant and taught his or her catechism and has taken the vows of confirmation moves more smoothly into the life of the church than the child who grows up in a church where adult conversions are sought as the norm. I doubt that the facts would bear this out. The United Church of Canada, for example, is currently engaged in vigorous dialogue about the meaning of baptism and church membership as well, reflecting the concern to make it more meaningful for parents and children alike.

Admittedly, the biblical basis for a view of solidarity and corporate guilt is debatable and uneven. We recognize that the "and their house" designation appears in the New Testament as well as the Old. It could be argued, against Jeremias and Cullmann, that the Old Testament prophetic voice tended to deny the corporate-guilt aspect and turned to individuality before God (Jeremiah 31:3). It is clear in the prophets that our children will suffer from our actions. And it is clear also that we need to be individually responsible before God. But does that deny that original sin is passed corporately through the human race and must also be dealt with in the new race, the church, whose Adam is Christ? We have moved too far in the direction of individualism. The Anabaptists recognized this danger and said that we must come before God for salvation *together*. At the same time, they rejected the practice of infant baptism. In so doing, they did not reject their children or in any sense make them feel that they were not part of the community of faith. To the contrary, they stated that children were clearly under God's grace and were "safe" until such time as they made other intentions clear. The authorities who persecuted the Anabaptist martyrs must have recognized implicitly that children were not responsible for their parents' behavior, nor were they part of the covenant commitment, because we do not read of any cases in which families were martyred that included children in that martyrdom.

Along with infant baptism, we must therefore also reject the notion of solidarity and the corpus Christianum which ensued from it. But we are still left with the question we raised earlier, "What is the place of children in the church?" Now we can rephrase the question and give it other substance. What would be a valid substitute for the concept of solidarity, which would make children and adolescents feel very much a part of the church, even before they became baptized members? Using the analogy of the family to speak of the church, it would be quite devastating to a child to be told that he or she is not really a part of the family, not until he or she can understand the meaning of "family." Just so, the young adolescent in the church, even after baptism, all too often feels more like "a church-member-in-training."

The fault for this, however, may not lie with our theology so much as with our attitudes and practices. Instead of emphasizing that the child is excluded at certain points, let us emphasize the places where the child is included and very much a part of the life of the congregation. Let me explain, using another analogy from family life. I perceive that, though I am not married all of my life, in retrospect, all of my life was a preparation for marriage. Nobody has yet bemoaned the fact that a child feels left out at a wedding, especially not if they are invited to the dinner! Four hundred and fifty-five years ago our forebears struggled to raise the standards of the church and church membership. Would we be fair to them or to our children to lower the standards today because someone might feel excluded? Quite to the contrary, we should maintain high standards and help our children reach them. That would present church membership as a particular challenge which they would joyfully anticipate. The fault, dear parents, is not in our children, but in us, if they feel left out. And changing the categories of meaning of baptism and church membership and communion will not answer those questions which we raised in this chapter.

If we feel a generation gap in the church, there are various points at which we can close the gap. Jesus showed us how, when he said, "Permit the little children to come to me, and do not forbid them." From childhood through adolescence we can and want to make our chidlren feel that they belong to the family of God. We can break down generation gaps by providing more creative forms of intergenerational activity in the congregation. Too often in our worship services, if we involve our children at all, we do it either by performing for them (we tell them exciting stories!) or by having them perform for us (they lisp cute children's songs in front of the congregation). But how often do we really worship together, at levels that we can all participate in and feel part of? There is much room for creative, careful planning in this area, and in all areas of church life, to include our children.

Let us return to the personal anecdote with which I began this chapter. If my experience as a youth is at all similar to what other youth today would like and need to experience, then we must find ways to integrate our congregational life with our social and other aspects of our lives. If we no longer have the advantages of natural communities, we must create community. Family groups in the congregation create opportunities for people to get to know each other better, including children and youth with adults. We may not all agree as to how important it is to create community; certainly we do not all agree how we should go about it and to what extent we can or ought to live communally. But I am speaking of regaining the sense of community which suggests that we have a real commitment to each other in the congregation, as real a commitment as we have to each other in the family. I think that John Driver, in *Community and Commitment*, is exactly right in stating that community and commitment belong together.

We are in a generation of individualism, in which people have mistakenly thought that their fulfillment must come in each one "doing his or her own thing." But when families start to break up and the very fabric of society seems threatened, we must surely learn the lesson that there is security and fulfillment in commitment to the community of faith. The best legacy we can provide our children is the one we have received—stable families in nurturing congregations. We can help our children and youth feel that they truly belong to the family of God.

Chapter Six

Youth as Members of the Church

We really do need each other! Mennonite youth belong to the church, and the church belongs to them. That has been affirmed throughout this study. We have simply attempted to distinguish appropriate expectations of the nature of their relationship to the church. In chapter five we affirmed their place in the church throughout the years of innocence. As Vernard Eller says, the church is like a camel caravan; it is going somewhere, and the adults are steering the camels. The children are very much part of the caravan. In fact, they are going to the same place the adults are going with the caravan. But they ride free. They do not yet steer their own camels! But all the time they observe the adults, and they will be better equipped to ride their own camels when the time comes.[26] We also emphasized the necessity for them to make conscious decisions as they become able to do so. These decisions are made with the full awareness of the implications of their sinful nature and tendency to rebel against the rule of God in their lives. These decisions are their responses to the call to a changed life and to be Jesus' disciples. They must decide to take their own stand before God. Then immediately, by choosing the Jesus way, they become part of the company of the committed. One does not become a Christian in isolation. If this is true for Christians generally, it is especially true and important for youth. They need our continued guidance as parents and adults in the congregation, so that they can grow free to make sound choices in their lives. None of us ever gets to the point that we do not need the advice and counsel of others. We, along with our youth, need each other as members of the church.

In this chapter we conclude our study by a brief examination of trends in the church regarding the participation of youth in church membership. We shall affirm the positive trends and suggest areas for improvement. In brief, we are all presented with the challenge of meaningful church membership for our youth in this generation.

Paul M. Lederach said in a *Builder* article: "We believe that baptism means entrance into the body of Christ, the fellowship of the saints, and giving and receiving of counsel, as well as the cleansing from sin and walking in newness of life."[27] I think that to be internally consistent, we should not baptize anyone to whom we are not willing to grant these rights and responsibilities. All too often adolescent baptism has meant (1) entrance into the church, but make decisions only at the youth group level, not on the congregational level; (2) entrance into the church, but study and fellowship primarily with people your own age; and (3) receive adult advice, but do not give any counsel in the fellowship of believers. Now if we believe that a fourteen-year-old is too young to make decisions in the congregation (example, by voting in business meetings), is he or she not in effect also too young to make the much greater decision of becoming a part of the kingdom of God? There has tended to be a discontinuity between our theology and our practice on this issue. Are we going to change our theology or our practice?

The question is the basic one of how we understand our covenant together in the church. I would like to call us back to the basics once again. In simple terms, baptism is the ceremony or symbol by which the individual enters into the covenant with God and the church of Jesus Christ. Communion is a regular covenant renewal ceremony. Both are to be practiced in the local congregation, or wherever there is a group of believers who consistently meet for Christian fellowship. Both are for those who have freely chosen, knowing the implications of their choice, to be part of the church of Christ. In that sense, both baptism and communion are exclusive rights belonging to those of mature status, not to children. Again, we must recognize that we cannot place maturity at an arbitrary or fixed age. But in an earlier chapter we attempted to define criteria by which we may ascertain maturity in terms of our development and our religious experience.

In the Mennonite Church, believer's baptism and believer's communion go together.[28] They help to provide a way to define those who are in the inner circle of church membership by personal choice and those who are part of the family of God by association. There may be other ceremonial or symbolic events which congregations use to mean the same thing. A variety in the practice of communion, baptism, and other symbolic events can be affirmed so long as they do not violate the central principle that there is a way to define those who are by choice members in the covenant community.

Now some people are still smarting under some rather artibrary practices of determining who are the "insiders" and the "outsiders" to the covenant. This is unfortunate. But this should not cause us to change our theology so much as it should cause us to reexamine some of our interpretations and applications of our views on the nature of the church and covenant. Defining the covenant should allow people a great sense of freedom. They know what is expected of them when they enter the covenant agreement in the congregation. They also have the freedom to remain outside the covenant, while still enjoying fellowship, worship, and study by their association with the community of faith. This gives them room enough and time to explore the meaning of Christian commitment and church membership from first-hand observation before they take that important step. This is, I think, a faithful model for nurture and evangelism in the life of the congregation. And this model is as equally valid for adults newly come into our midst as it is for our youth who have grown up in our midst. The result will be a stronger, more informed commitment, resulting in healthier congregations.

To use the word "authority" in a discussion of the life of a congregation is like saying "boo"; it scares people! But it should be seen as a positive word. From its roots, it means simply caring for that which one "authors" or creates. In a positive sense, parents have authority over the children whom they have "authored" or brought into the world. It is considered healthy in the life of the biological family when the roles of parents and children are not diffused or confused. Is it not a prevalent sickness in our contemporary society that parents find it difficult to assert their proper positive authority? And has this sickness not also infiltrated the church, the spiritual family? If we older people regain a sense of the meaning of being church, if we learn how to commit ourselves to Christ and to each other in meaningful and explicit ways with warmth, integrity, love, and mutual submission, we shall have come a long way toward resolving our youths' problem with us!

The tension is not so much between youth and adults as it is between the "ongoingness" of the church and its "first generation" qualities, that new vitality which must be infused in each new generation. This is in a real sense the "burden of Anabaptism" which we have to bear. We are not satisfied to perpetuate a "folk religion" by which people drift in and out of the church from generation to generation. We want to keep the conscious choices always before us and our youth. For that reason, the tension is a healthy tension and a key ingredient in keeping us growing as Christians and as a denomination.

Now, in youth there is always the tension between their great idealism and the realities which they face around them. The church needs youth to continue to highlight and sharpen this tension. Adults become too pragmatic and sometimes a bit lethargic all too soon. We need youth in the church because they see visions. We need the elderly in the church because they dream dreams and help us to remember where we came from. We definitely need each other.

In a study of this kind, one tends to work with impressions too much and not enough with facts. The most recent churchwide study which was done that is relevant to us here is the Harder-Kauffman Church Membership Profile, completed in 1972 and published as *Anabaptists Four Centuries Later*, by Herald Press. This study covers five constituent groups of the Mennonite Central Committee in North America.

In the fourth chapter, Leland Harder evaluates the test results of "the variables of church participation." He first cites the 1963 census figures. In that year the median age of baptism breaks down as follows: Those over fifty years old reported having been baptized at 16.5 years, those 30 to 49, at 14.5 years, and those 20 to 29, at 13.6 years, for an overall average of 14.9 years. Note especially the trend toward a younger age for baptism. In the 1972 study, the median age in the Mennonite Church is 14.0. There is then an overall decline in age of baptism of almost three years, based on the reporting of the older age-group, to today. Remember, lest you conclude that 14 years is an acceptable age to be baptized, that there are as many younger as older than that. Conversion, which usually comes before baptism, occurred at a median age of 13.6 years overall, 12.8 years for those between ages 20 to 29 who reported. In other words, many people in recent years in the Mennonite Church have been twelve or less at the time of conversion, some as young as six, seven, or eight. In any case, the broad consensus is that as of 1972, 95 percent of all conversions in the Mennonite Church occurred before age 17.

There has been a more recent, albeit much smaller, survey done in the Mennonite Conference of Ontario in 1979. This study may be somewhat indicative of more recent trends. In the period April 1977 to March 1979, there were 228 persons baptized in Mennonite Conference of Ontario congregations, after an initial commitment to Christ. This information is based on questionnaires sent to pastors, with 84 percent responding. The youngest was 11, the oldest 76, and the median age of baptism was 17.5. This indicates a distinct upswing in the age of baptism and membership of youth in the Mennonite Church, in Ontario at least. It is significant to note a further breakdown of the figures. There were only 8 persons baptized under 12 years old, 59 at 13 to 15 years, 86 at 16 to 18 years, 25 at 19 to 21 years, 19 at 22 to 24 years, and 40 persons 25 years old or older. As was noted in chapter one, the home, church membership classes, and public meetings ranked highest as settings in which persons made their commitments to Christ. Mennonite Youth Fellowship (MYF) ranked seventh, after small groups, Sunday school, and camp settings.[29]

This last fact brings us to a discussion of the place of MYF in the church and the place of our youth in the youth fellowship. It has been noted, in Ontario at last, that the upper age limit for participation in Mennonite Youth Fellowship is on a steady decline. It appears that relatively few youth stay with MYF after high school. Much of this is as a result of college and careers which take them away from the home congregations. But not entirely. Of course, there has also developed the "college and careers" groups as a kind of "senior MYF." How do these facts and impressions fit together? Note first of all that in Ontario the median age for baptism and church membership is right at the point of the person's senior year in high school. Some make their commitments during their earlier high school years. That means that they will be part of the MYF for four years or less, *as church members*. In terms of our nurture program in the congregation, we can no longer assume that the people in our MYF Sunday school classes are Christians. We must nurture with evangelism in mind! A second observation is that we must be certain that our youth continue to have their faith nurtured beyond high school and MYF years. We must find ways to integrate them into the life of our congregations between the years 17 to 25, possibly the most crucial years in Christian nurture endeavors today. Our youth are very much in transition, and we can hardly keep up with what is happening to them. Between the Harder-Kauffman study and today, *two generations of MYFers* have passed through our congregations!

It is self-evident that our youth, and for that matter all of our members, prefer and need at times to relate to persons their own age. Peer group needs are most predominant in the adolescent years. MYF was formed to fill those social and spiritual needs of youth. MYF filled a gap in our church program. Now we must be careful that the pendulum does not swing too far the other way. Let us not make MYF into a "para-church" organization like Sunday school once was. Let us not "slice and dice" our congregations into arbitrary groupings based on age and sex, married and single status, etc. If the model of the church as the family of God has any validity, then we must work toward integration and holistic approaches in our congregational life. It is helpful when MYF groups plan dinners with senior citizens, or when MYFers and parents have occasional joint events. Let these not be mere tokens, but let them reflect an ongoing interdependence and mutuality in the life the congregation.

Youth as church members should be given opportunity to exercise *all* the rights, privileges, and responsibilites of church membership, including voting and holding offices and giving to the budget. But let us do away with tokenism. There should be MYFers on church committees, not because we have a spot to fill, but because of their gifts as perceived in the congregation. The gifts of our youth as well as adults need to be affirmed and developed. Could we devise positions on all committees of "participant-observers," who would sit on committees for a year before becoming fully-functional members of the committee? This would not be to single out the youth once again, but to recognize that there are many latent gifts in congregations *among young and old alike,* which could be developed with a bit of nurturing. Once our youth choose baptism and church membership, they should no longer be viewed as "the church of tomorrow." They are very much a part of the church today.

In conclusion, let us make several affirmations. Our children are as much a part of the church as they are a part of our families. We simply do not teach them beyond what they are able to understand, nor do we expect them to make decisions which are involuntary or inappropriate to their ability to follow through. *We allow children to be children!* There are rights and responsibilities which belong to them. These do not necessarily or at all points include the rights and responsibilities of church membership.

Baptism and church membership belong together. Baptism is a symbolic act by which people witness to their decision to enter into the covenant of grace before God and with each other in the church. The rights and responsibilities which proceed from this covenant agreement must be worked out in each generation, based on Scripture, historical theology, and on a lively contemporary process of giving and receiving counsel in the church. This process is suited to mature persons who can choose of their own volition to be part of the process. Our youth may be expected to be part of that process when they are willing and capable of being part of it.

We nurture our youth toward responsible decision-making in all areas of life, including spiritual life. Our task is not to water down the essential meaning of baptism and church membership, communion and worship, and everything else we hold to be important so that we reach the lowest common denominator. Rather, we nurture and educate our children so that after they reach the age of accountability they may be ready to give an account of themselves and make the faith their own. Mennonite youth belong to the church, and the church belongs to them. Let us help them to take hold of their wonderful inheritance!

Notes

1. Charles William Stewart, *Adolescent Religion: A Developmental Study of the Religion of Youth* (Abingdon Press, New York, 1967).

2. Harold S. Bender, *These Are My People* (Herald Press, Scottdale, Pa., 1962).

3. For further exposition along these lines, read the provocative book by Vernard Eller, *In Place of Sacraments* (Eerdmans, Grand Rapids, 1972).

4. John H. Yoder, ed. and transl. *The Schleitheim Confession* (Herald Press, Scottdale, Pa., 1977), pp. 11 and 25.

5. Dirk Philips, *Hand Book* (Pathway Publishers, Aylmer, Ontario, 1966), p. 17.

6. This view of Matthew 19:14 (cf. Mark 10:14) is by no means the only possible interpretation of that verse, but serves our purposes here and is plausible.

7. Some would suggest that it is a misnomer to speak of children being "safe" or "saved." They have no need to be saved because they have no guilt. Frank Schiemer, a sixteenth-century Anabaptist, would tend to this view. Much depends on how one views original sin, whether a child is in fact guilty at birth or not. In any case, for purposes of this discussion, the outcome is the same. In Christ all is well for the innocent child who has not yet chosen consciously to rebel against his Maker.

8. Rollin S. Armour, *Anabaptist Baptism* (Herald Press, Scottdale, Pa., 1966), pp. 27ff. See also Paul K. Jewett, *Infant Baptism and the Covenant of Grace* (Eerdmans, Grand Rapids, 1978) for a further exposition of this theme.

9. John Funk, *Martyrs Mirror* (Sohm edition, 1886), pp. 1029, 932, 1061 respectively.

10. Gordon W. Allport, *Becoming* (Macmillan, New York, 1961).

11. Erik Erikson, *Childhood and Society* (Norton, New York, 1964).

12. John Drescher, *Seven Things Children Need* (Herald Press, Scottdale, Pa., 1976), p. 140, who also quotes *Sex Education* (Sacred Design, 1968).

13. Gordon W. Allport, *The Individual and His Religion* Macmillan, New York, 1961), p. 52.

14. Gideon Yoder, *The Nurture and Evangelism of Children* (Herald Press, Scottdale, Pa., 1959).

15. Allport, *Becoming* p. 1.

16. Allport, *Becoming*, p. 79.

17. Allport, *Becoming*, p. 73.

18. S. J. DeVries, *The Interpreter's Dictionary of the Bible*, IV (Abingdon, New York, 1962), p. 362.

19. William James, *The Varieties of Religious Experience* Collier Books, N.Y., 1970), p. 160.

20. Harder, Leland, and Howard Kauffman, *Anabaptists Four Centuries Later* (Herald Press, Scottdale, Pa., 1974), p. 10.

21. James, *The Varieties of Religious Experience*, p. 168, who also quotes E. D. Starbuck, *The Psychology of Religion*, pp. 224, 262.

22. James, *The Varieties of Religious Experience*, p. 167.

23. J. C. Wenger, *Introduction to Theology* (Herald Press, Scottdale, Pa., 1954), p. 282, who also quotes Menno Simons.

24. G. R. Beasley-Murray, *Baptism in the New Testament* (Eerdmans, Grand Rapids, 1973), ch. 1, to whom I am indebted for material in this section.

25. For this and related information, I am indebted to *Encyclopedia Judaica*, IV, pp. 244 ff.

26. Vernard Eller, *In Place of Sacraments* (Eerdmans, Grand Rapids, 1972).

27. Paul M. Lederach, "The Meaning of Church Membership," in *The Builder*, June 1978 (Mennonite Publishing House, Scottdale, Pa.) and Faith and Life Press, Newton, Kan.

28. See also the arguments put forth by Paul K. Jewett in *Infant Baptism and the Covenant of Grace* (Eerdmans, Grand Rapids, 1978), pp. 201-207.

29. From an unpublished survey questionnaire designed by Carol Shantz, Faith and Life Committee, Mennonite Conference of Ontario.

Bibliography

Allport, Gordon W. *Becoming*. New York: Macmillan, 1961.
_____ *The Individual and His Religion*. New York: Macmillan, 1961.
Armour, Rollin S. *Anabaptist Baptism*. Scottdale, Pa.: Herald Press, 1966.
Babin, Pierre. *Crisis of Faith*. New York: Herder and Herder, 1963.
Beasley-Murray, G. R. *Baptism in the New Testament*. Grand Rapids: Eerdmans, 1973.
DeVries, S. J. "Sin, Sinners," *The Interpreters' Dictionary of the Bible*, Vol. IV. New York: Abingdon, 1962.
Drescher, John M. *Seven Things Children Need*. Scottdale, Pa.: Herald Press, 1976.
Driver, John. *Community and Commitment*. Scottdale, Pa.: Herald Press, 1976.
Eller, Vernard. *In Place of Sacraments*. Grand Rapids: Eerdmans, 1972.
Encylcopedia Judaica, Vol. IV. New York: Macmillan.
Erickson, Erik. *Childhood and Society*. New York: Norton, 1964.
Freud, Sigmund and Oskar Pfister, ed. Heinrich Meng and Ernst L. Freud, trans. Eric Mosbacher. *Psychoanalysis and Faith*.

New York: Basic Books, 1963.

Friedmann, Robert. *The Theology of Anabaptism*. Scottdale, Pa.: Herald Press, 1973.

Fromm, Erich. *Psychoanalysis and Religion*. Clinton, Mass.: Yale Paperbound, Colonial Press, 1959.

Funk, John ed. *Martyrs Mirror*. Sohm edition, 1886.

Gish, Arthur G. *Living in Christian Community*. Scottdale, Pa.: Herald Press, 1979.

Harder, Leland and Howard Kauffman. *Anabaptists Four Centuries Later*. Scottdale, Pa.: Herald Press, 1974.

James, William. *The Varieties of Religious Experience*. New York: Collier Books, 1961.

Jersild, Arthur T. *The Psychology of Adolescence*. New York: Macmillan, 1978.

Jewett, Paul K. *Infant Baptism and the Covenant of Grace*. Grand Rapids: Eerdmans, 1978.

Lederach, Paul. *Mennonite Youth*. Scottdale, Pa.: Herald Press, 1971.

_____. "The Meaning of Church Membership," *Builder*, Scottdale, Pa.: Mennonite Publishing House and Newton, Kan.: Faith and Life Press, June 1978.

Lehn, Cornelia. *The Education and Conversion of Children*. Newton, Kan.: Faith and Life Press.

Stewart, Charles W. *Adolescent Religion: A Development Study of the Religion of Youth*. New York: Abingdon, 1967.

Vitz, Paul C. *Psychology as Religion*. Grand Rapids: Eerdmans, 1977.

Westerhoff, John H. III. *Will Our Children Have Faith?* Garden City, N.Y.: Seabury Press, 1976.

Yoder, Gideon G. *The Nurture and Evangelism of Children*. Scottdale, Pa.: Herald Press, 1959 (op).

Yoder, John H., ed. *The Schleitheim Confession*. Scottdale, Pa.: Herald Press, 1977.

THE FOCAL PAMPHLET SERIES

1. *Integration! Who's Prejudiced?*
   by C. Norman Kraus, (1958). OP
2. *The Church and the Community,*
   by Lawrence Burkholder (1958). OP
3. *The Ecumenical Movement and the Faithful Church,*
   by John H. Yoder (1959). OP
4. *Biblical Revelation and Inspiration,*
   by Harold S. Bender (1959).
5. *As You Go,* by John H. Yoder (1961). OP
6. *The Christian Calling,* by Virgil Vogt (1961). OP
7. *The Price of Church Unity,* by Harold E. Bauman (1962). OP
8. *Television: Friend or Foe?* by Henry Weaver (1962). OP
9. *Brotherhood and Schism,* by Calvin Redekop (1963). OP
10. *The Call to Preach,* by Clayton Beyler (1963). OP
11. *The Church Functions with Purpose,*
    by Calvin Redekop (1967).
12. *Let's Talk About Extremism,* by Edgar Metzler (1968). OP
13. *Helping Developing Countries,* by Carl Kreider
    (1968). OP
14. *The Christian Stance in a Revolutionary Age,*
    by Donald R. Jacobs (1968).
15. *Pacifism and Biblical Nonresistance,*
    by J. C. Wenger (1968).

FOCAL PAMPHLETS treat timely subjects of special Christian interest
and concern. They interpret and discuss problems of contemporary life as
they relate to Christian truth.

Each addition to the series attempts to bring the life and thought of the
Christian community into focus on a specific issue. Each pamphlet
presents a valid viewpoint, but not necessarily the final word or the official
position of the publisher or his constituency.

Some Focal Pamphlets grow out of intense personal study and research.
Others are first prepared for presentation at special conferences or
professional meetings.

The series will continue as suitable manuscripts become available.

Maurice Martin was born in rural Waterloo County, Ontario, Canada, in 1946. He remained there until he reached his early twenties.

Martin received a BA from the University of Waterloo, Waterloo, Ontario; a secondary schoolteacher's certificate from Althouse College of Education; and a Master of Divinity degree from the Goshen Biblical Seminary, Elkhart, Indiana. His seminary studies included a year of supervised pastoral education in London, Ontario.

Martin is pastor of the Hagerman Mennonite Church, Milliken, Ontario, located near Toronto. He served as an assistant pastor of the Elmira Mennonite Church for two years. Earlier he taught English in the secondary school system in Hamilton, Ontario, for three years. In addition to his congregational responsibilities Martin serves as secretary of the Faith and Life Committee of the Mennonite Conference of Ontario and chairs the board of the Markham Family Life Centre.

Maurice and Phyllis (Shantz) Martin are parents of two children, Benjamin and Joelle.